Refreshing Comms truly captures th᠎ communication within an organization. It eloquently emphasises the vital significance of comprehending the unique needs and motivations of our employees, showcasing how forging this connection can bring about remarkable transformations. As the lifeblood of any company, people are at the heart of success, and this book illustrates how the way we communicate with them can have a profound impact.

The book highlights the pivotal role internal communication plays as a building block in fostering enduring and profound relationships between individuals and the organizations they serve.

What sets *Refreshing Comms* apart is its ability to present complex concepts in a refreshingly accessible manner. The author's writing style is engaging and relatable, making it easy for readers of all backgrounds to grasp the concepts and apply them in real-world scenarios.

Jennifer Sproul, Chief Executive,
Institute of Internal Communication

Refreshing Comms is a fitting title for a book that really does offer a fresh, accessible guide to mastering the art of employee communication.

It bridges the gap between theory and practice, offering a wealth of practical tools, templates, techniques and insights. Use this as a hands-on guide for confidently navigating today's complex employee comms landscape.

In short, *Refreshing Comms* is a breath of fresh air in the literature on internal communication.

Katie Macaulay, MD of AB Communications Ltd, author, lecturer and board member of The International Association of Business Communicators

There's nothing but good, powerful and useful things on EVERY page. Liz has done herself and the IC profession proud with a smartly produced, accessible book. A 'whispering scream' for more powerful, connecting and clear internal communication. If you want to get corporate comms right, start and end with this book. It'll serve you well.

Perry Timms, HR's Most Influential Thinker 2022 and Founder & Chief Energy Officer, PTHR

Global forces are converging to create increasing complexity in the way we organize ourselves at work. To cut through ambiguity, organizations need to connect all internal stakeholders to their business strategy and vision. It's incumbent on every leader of every organization to prioritize communication for internal clarity and alignment. *Refreshing Comms* is a no-nonsense, easy-to-read guide for internal communication excellence and every business should have a copy.

Cat Barnard, Director, Working the Future

Internal communication for a better-connected, feel-good, goal-achieving workplace

Refreshing Comms

Liz Atkin

First published in Great Britain by Practical Inspiration Publishing, 2024

© Atkin, 2024

The moral rights of the author have been asserted

ISBN   978-1-78860-585-4 (hardback)
       978-1-78860-543-4 (paperback)
       978-1-78860-545-8 (epub)
       978-1-78860-544-1 (mobi)

Every effort has been made to trace copyright holders and to obtain their permission for the use of copyright material. The publisher apologizes for any errors or omissions and would be grateful if notified of any corrections that should be incorporated in future reprints or editions of this book.

Want to bulk-buy copies of this book for your team and colleagues? We can customize the content and co-brand *Refreshing Comms* to suit your business's needs.

Please email info@practicalinspiration.com for more details.

Practical Inspiration
Publishing

To my mum – I miss you.

Contents

Foreword

Communication is the fundamental component, the golden thread, that runs through everything. It is representative of culture, it is the articulation of the strategy and it's what we need to function as a group or community.

This is how I have always talked about the power of communication inside organizations, so when I read 'As a leader or manager in any profession, internal communication is the most powerful tool you can employ in the workplace' in *Refreshing Comms*, I knew that it was going to be a book that could really enable change for anyone leading an organization.

What makes internal communication so challenging is the breadth of it. Every organization manages it differently and this means the resource, skills and time allocated to it varies wildly. Thankfully, more research is being done and *Refreshing Comms* highlights some recent work from 2023 that explores employee perspectives on internal communication as well as perspectives from others in the profession.

The pandemic has left leaders and organizations in chaos, and focusing efforts to improve communication will make a huge difference to engagement, efficiencies and the employee experience. What Liz does in this book, is provide the perfect framework for you to follow to create the communication strategy and plan for your organization. She brings simplicity, humour and ease to the topic making it easy to navigate with a practical example to follow throughout.

The step-by-step guide to completing Liz's Tools of Engagement Framework, the practical advice on writing better content to engage your employees and the simplicity of combining different parts of an organization will enable you to sit and plan your internal communication with intention.

It's this insight that allows you to gain a deeper understanding of the need to invest in communication and these insights are peppered throughout the book in relevant chapters to bring to life that importance.

Liz's career has been a journey of leadership and learning. Her experience leading organizations in different sectors means that she has seen the impact of poor communication, challenging cultures and the difficulty of business improvement. As we chatted about the book, she told me that she felt her career was one that had so many different directions it doesn't naturally lend itself to writing this book. But that's what makes it different and it's what makes it usable for anyone leading teams or organizations today.

As I read the book on trains, at home and in a tent in Scotland, I was struck by the practicality of it. I've scribbled notes on it and used it with clients already to help them understand the intricacies of things like employer branding, messaging and employee engagement.

When you've been working in the profession for over 20 years you can feel like there isn't much you don't know when it comes to the frameworks and fundamentals of internal communication. But this book brought forward some additional tools, insights and discussion points that everyone in communication, HR and operations should take the time to read. For those organizations who lack the resource in internal communication, this is your handbook for creating a plan to take your employees with you, wherever you might be going.

Jenni Field, Communications Strategist, Founder and CEO of Redefining Communications, author and speaker

Introduction

What does it take to write internal communications that persuade people to buy into your way of thinking? How do you go about making your case? And more to the point, why won't people just do what you want them to do? Well, wonder no more because you're about to find out!

Applying a simple but smart mix of ingredients – winning marketing strategy, psychology and proven writing formulas – this book will help you win in a way you haven't before. It gives you a communication framework model, complete with tools, customizable blank templates and working examples, along with all the essential human context and insightful know-how you need to refresh your comms – and your thinking.

There's even top tips, thought bubbles and practical exercises to help get you really invested in becoming a better communicator.

I've written this book to be an easy read with its own personality as a demo in itself of how it's possible to get really important business stuff across without resorting to textbook management speak and oodles of charts and data. So, I hope it also acts as an inspiring example as well as a guide.

Shining a spotlight on the obvious, but often ignored fact that even verbally delivered information starts life as words prepared on paper (or screen), *Refreshing Comms* focuses predominantly on the must-have leadership and management competency of effective *written* communication.

As well as being your everyday strategic partner for employee engagement, internal communication is starting to receive a lot more attention as a mighty management tool.

Whatever you believe employee engagement to be, it's at the top of the employer agenda right now for many credible reasons, from staff retention to its effects on the bottom line. You can see employee engagement being taken more seriously in lots of ways, including subtle changes in terminology, with roles such as 'Head of HR' being retitled 'Head of People and Culture' (which incidentally is a great example of how a simple change in word choice can shift meaning and focus – lots more on this little gem in the book!). Across reports, surveys and of course lived experience, evidence is being captured that a 'soft revolution' in the workplace is underway, and a shift in employer thinking, communication and behaviour is needed in response.

Inevitably, even with the best will in the world many professionals in leadership, management and indeed HR find themselves just too busy with operational planning, daily tasks and compliance to be able to step into the role of strategic communicator. And many SMEs simply don't have the benefit of their own dedicated HR department, let alone an internal communication team.

So, if you're thinking 'How can I possibly sort out internal communications in this organization? I don't have any credentials!' think again. I mean that may be so technically, but what I'd like to point out is that you care enough to read this book because you *know* things could be much better. Which means what you *can* do is take great communication advice and set about applying it to your workplace for the benefit of everyone (including yourself) step by step.

Whether you want to improve your existing internal communication strategy or create one from scratch, you'll find all the impetus, rationale, know-how and solutions you need to plan and write internal communications with wisdom and skill. And with that nailed, you and your senior team will be in a far more favourable and sustainable position to help your employees adapt, evolve and get behind your business goals, whatever the prevailing wind.

The original power tool

As a leader or manager in any profession, internal communication is *the* most powerful tool you can employ in the workplace, especially in times when your organization is dealing with major change and you need to keep your people on board, feeling secure and motivated.

You could describe communication as a pretty easy thing to do. Just open your mouth and the words come out. Grab a sticky note and scribble. Tickle the keyboard and hey presto, an email. On the other hand, hindsight can show it to be a bit of a tricky thing to get right. Realizing you've said something in the wrong way or in the wrong tone and then backtracking isn't a great way to operate. And you can end up creating misunderstandings, niggling people and lighting little fires here and there that you've then got to spend precious time putting out.

Like any tool, it's only as good as the people who use it. At the very least, communicators need to be clear about what they're saying to who and why. If a message or request is dismissed as irrelevant, gets misunderstood or fails to achieve the desired response, then the tool has fallen short of its potential. It's simply being used poorly.

Used like a mallet, communication is just a blunt instrument, capable only of producing crude results. Used more precisely like a fine chisel, it can help carve out the best of outcomes.

So, what drove me to write this particular book?

I love people and I love business. Not a particularly ground-breaking set of interests I grant you, but gaining an understanding of how both typically operate and influence each other, has taught me a great deal over the years about communication. Stuff that I feel compelled to put into the pages of this book and share with you.

My baptism of fire with internal communication came about the very first time I was in charge of a whole organization – responsible as CEO for strategy, operations, finances and people. I soon realized that implementing change, even for the most critical of reasons (like trying to save people's jobs and keep services running), can be a pretty tough gig. Especially when you find you've inherited a culture that reveals itself to be the opposite of what you thought it was and is definitely nowhere near what you're trying to create. Though I was thrilled at the challenge and never shy of hard work, that job still ranks as the most difficult experience of my career. But thankfully there was a silver lining – I learned a valuable lesson from my initial naivety. It was this: You can't assume that just because people show up at work every day that they're somehow as fired up as you are about the company's vision and future aspirations. Not even if your super-duper, commercially-sound vision statement is hung on every wall flashing in neon lights (it wasn't by the way) and you spend more time than is sensible talking your patient backside off (which I did) trying to get all kinds of different disgruntled people engaged, on-board and on-brand.

Later in my career (once I'd recovered!) I went on to spend almost ten years learning about and working in business improvement and culture change – I know, ironic right? During this time, I visited and spoke with leaders and managers of hundreds of manufacturing and service-based companies of various shapes and sizes, all falling foul of poor communication, no matter how many shiny new, fandangled (love that word) digital messaging channels or devices they adopted.

Since then, of course, the COVID-19 pandemic and its subsequent knock-on effects has forced the rethinking and design of internal communication, driven by a growing understanding of its direct influence on organizational wellbeing, good employee experience and business success.

There's still a need for capturing new ways and different approaches for doing it better and this book plays its part by showing you not only *why*, but also *how* to get the absolute most out of your internal comms, your people and by de facto your business.

Even now, as I run my own B2B business I'm often astonished at the lack of thought put into communications by some organizations, creating situations that end up with everyone blaming each other when things get misunderstood or mistakes happen.

Typically, it's only the retrospective look back at the effort of implementing change and the subsequent results that teaches you that the better the communication, the easier the change. Seems like such an obvious statement doesn't it? But knowing it to be true and adjusting your own actions accordingly are two entirely different things.

So, here's a fresh approach to thinking about, and then tackling, the challenge of getting your message across in a way that hits different and is practical enough to be used by *any* organization keen to succeed.

How this book works

The primary purpose of *Refreshing Comms* is to deepen your understanding and add to your skill set by improving the way you communicate in such a way that you'll always then have the ability to use the power of words, tone and language for creating the kind of meaningful communication that leads to positive outcomes.

At the heart of *Refreshing Comms* is my 'Tools of Engagement Framework' which conveniently brings together everything you need to be highly effective.

Using a fictional business as a working example, we'll complete each element of this practical Framework template in turn. And chapter by chapter, I'll share with you the reasons why and the means of how you can customize and put into action your own Tools of Engagement Framework in your organization.

The first two chapters provide the context. You'll:

- discover what internal communication is all about and why, more than ever, you need to be good at it;
- delve into the *real* narrative of what goes in the workplace; and
- understand what makes people tick.

Then from chapter three onwards, you'll:

- be introduced to the Tools of Engagement Framework and see a working example created, chapter by chapter, so you can go on to customize your own;
- learn how my Rules of Engagement and Hallmarks of High Value Content hold the key to effective, strategic comms;
- uncover professional writing techniques and strategies that'll have you writing like a pro!;
- consider how best to define and measure the value of internal communications; and
- take some time for reflection on what you've read and how you can use it to make a difference.

Applying any new plan or approach will always take time and consideration in the beginning. But before you know it, this Framework will become a natural part of your communication planning, writing and delivery, helping you to translate business goals into intentional messages that hold both commercial purpose and human meaning.

I want you to enjoy this book. I want you to be able to use it to help your people and the organization you're all a part of to develop, advance and enjoy new possibilities through better connection and better results. Read it, share it, put it into action. There's nothing to lose and everything to gain.

Chapter 1

What's this internal communication thing *really* about?

Good question! It sounds obvious at first blush, but then when you try and define exactly what it is, you see how tricky it becomes because it influences pretty much everything.

Before we get stuck in, here's a quick bit of housekeeping: 'internal communication' is a bit of a mouthful (even if you're not reading out loud!) so for the purposes of sticking to my promise that this is an easy-read book, and appreciating how busy you are, I'll sometimes refer to it as IC or internal comms. Much better.

Ok, so where were we? Definitions. There's actually no one singular definition of internal comms. And that's not surprising because it's become a hugely broad and multifaceted field that touches on many disciplines as we begin to take learning from elsewhere and recognize its relevant application in today's workplace.

The HR profession alone has grown by 42% in the past decade compared to just 10% for the general workforce according to the Chartered Institute of Personnel and Development

(CIPD) latest UK people profession update. At the time of writing, the CIPD itself recognizes 12 defined career areas for people professionals with dedicated remits such as employee engagement, people and culture and employee experience – all of which have differences but require a sound understanding and application of communication.

If you look at the Institute of Internal Communication (IoIC) definition they say:

> 'At the most basic level, you have to communicate well at the right time so employees know what is expected of them and what is happening in the organization. At a deeper level, for employees to feel engaged with their workplace and give their best, they have to see that their organization cares about their views and understand how their role contributes towards overall business objectives.'

Absolutely right too. But how do you, in your role as a busy leader or people manager – without any dedicated internal comms resource or specific strategy to draw on – unpick that and turn it into something cohesive and practical for everyday use that actually has the desired effect?

Until recent times, the impact of IC on businesses had only been studied at an academic level which wasn't particularly inviting or accessible for non-experts to explore, discover and learn. Fortunately, we're now far better informed and aware of how things are evolving and what it means today for organizations of all types and sizes.

Through its State of the Sector, Internal Communication and Employee Experience reports, global consultancy group Gallagher has been actively reporting the year-on-year evolution of IC and anticipating the trends that lie ahead.

Their report headline for the focus of IC in 2023 is 'recalibration'. It states:

> 'The scope of internal communication continues to expand into all areas of organizational wellbeing, culture and employee experience, putting under-resourced teams under considerable pressure.'

Similar to previous years, is that internal comms continues to be a vastly undervalued and underutilized tool (and let's be honest, skill) yet to be discovered and harnessed by many organizations. Even though it doesn't feature as an asset on your balance sheet, it sure as heck influences it. And here's the thing – when used well, it'll do much of the heavy lifting for you, even when you're busy elsewhere. Keep that thought in mind!

During the writing of this book, the IoIC published its IC Index 2023 report produced in conjunction with Ipsos Karian and Box, a strategic insight and innovative reporting agency. The study asked employees – rather than employers – across the UK what they want and need from internal communications.

Its findings provide rich context, giving much credibility to this book's purpose. So, let's take a moment to digest a few highlights.

In its introduction, the report states:

> 'We need honest, reliable communications now more than ever.'

It goes on to pose a number of key, fundamental questions triggered by its findings such as:

> 'How do we help leaders communicate in a way that inspires trust?'

> 'How do we talk about change?'

These are brilliant questions that we'll tackle head-on in this book.

Among the study's top take-aways:

- There are still large groups of employees who are either negative, confused or unconvinced about the quality of internal communication.
- In terms of topics, people rank as a priority more clear and authentic information on how their employer organization is *performing*, what the business *priorities* and *team goals* are and what *progress* is being made.
- Employees are spending very little time reading and viewing updates; most spend just 15 minutes or less per day doing this.
- While innovation has its place, most people (55%) prefer written communication and favour the more traditional routes of email.

- Workers describing poor communication use words such as: scripted, formal, uninspired, unclear, boring and meaningless.
- Staff surveys alone won't get the job done. Regular listening and manager feedback are essential for hitting high levels of positivity.
- Dedicated internal communication teams make a positive difference.

The last point is welcome and promising and shows how important a role internal communication has. But what if you're not fortunate enough to have an IC team for whatever reason, what are your options then?

And what's in store for 2024 and beyond? Well, we'll wait to see what the research and surveys report to us in due course. But a quick glance into the future already reveals the conference agenda topics that are going to be taking centre stage. Among them:

- Rebalancing relationships and addressing 'The Great Resignation'.
- Strategies to nurture culture and a sense of belonging.
- Developing and delivering consistent messaging across channels and departments to avoid miscommunication.
- Keeping communication open and transparent to build honest relationships.
- Strategies and resources for communicating with a divided, blended and dispersed workforce.
- Integration of thinking models from change management, learning, and communications design.

- Embedding a clear and informative internal communications strategy.
- Using internal communications to champion diversity, equity and inclusion
- Avoiding communication overload.

Lots to consider for all employers.

Where and how does communication take place?

Communication happens everywhere all of the time. But that's not a very helpful statement when you're trying to 'catch it', optimize it and make it work better for everyone. And there's both the verbal and written kinds to get right.

Verbal communication is by nature immediate (discounting recorded messages of course). It's 'in and of the moment' and happens either face to face, phone to phone or screen to screen. There's going to be potential for instant questions and feedback in these verbal scenarios, so when you're the conversation initiator you'll want to be clear on what you're going to say, why you're saying it and how you frame your message. You'll also want to know that the message has been understood and that any questions have been asked and answered as far as possible at that point – and that means listening.

As for the written word, this is where the real power lies – and this will become more obvious as a major point throughout the book. Written words have to be even more thoughtfully chosen than those in a face-to-face conversation. Mainly because when you're face to face you can see the other person responding to you in real time, like nodding along, frowning if they're not sure of something or dare I say, glazing over! And as well as their body language, you can gauge the intonation in their voice to interpret how they're feeling or reacting. Which is handy because you can always make adjustments to help moderate the conversation if needed.

Also, verbal communication isn't usually remembered word for word, and worse, can get lost in translation when passed on – the cause of many a misunderstanding. The written word though hangs around long after the message has been sent and received, and as such stays there in black and white with nowhere to hide!

Either digital or in print, here's a few of the most common forms of written communication in the workplace:

- mission statement, vision statement, values, business goals;
- company announcements (the good and the not so good);
- emails;
- meeting agendas and minutes;
- newsletters;
- internal reports;
- staff handbooks;
- instructions (e.g., operating procedures);
- induction manuals; and
- job ads and job descriptions.

Each of these offer a golden opportunity to make a positive connection that sets the right tone from the start. Let me give you a great example with the following, posted by an employee on LinkedIn who was motivated to share his experience with his network by genuine surprise and joy:

> 'Just got a calendar invite from my boss titled "quick chat – good thing" and I've never been more grateful/ impressed with anyone in my life. A workplace revolutionary tbh.'

As much as I love this (as did others who reposted it) I couldn't help but feel sad that this guy's reaction shows just how rare and unusual it is for a boss to say the right thing in the right way. Even if it's just asking someone to a meeting in a way that puts them at ease. I mean, it's not rocket science is it? And moreover, it'll have taken his boss a nanosecond to do, but the impact on that guy – legend.

Whose job is it anyway?

Internal communication is a hard thing to pin down. Whose responsibility is it? HR, PR, marketing? Fluttering around like a butterfly but never quite settling anywhere, it's just a free spirit that means well but often misjudges how to land a message that gets the desired response.

Communicating is part of every manager's role, but internal communication as a management function is a relatively new discipline – incredibly undervalued at a time when, ironically, the need for improved employer-employee relationships has never been more glaringly obvious or acute. So, inevitably it's just picked up on the fly as you go along.

The ITPR report 'How Good (or Bad) are UK Businesses at Communicating with their Employees' (2022) looked at the state of IC in businesses with 100+ employees.

By interviewing decision-makers in HR, marketing and communication roles, it produced some interesting findings, such as even when there's an agreed understanding of where IC sits and whose job it is, there are still flaws that remain. And they found issues caused by the very different styles of communication from colleagues working in different departments.

Messaging from HR is typically more process focused – understandably so given the level of compliance often involved. Comms that come purely through the marketing department tend to come across too 'salesy' and strike the wrong chords internally. PR (if you even have a PR department) can be too far removed with a predominantly external focus, and comms from executive and governance quarters are typically too high level, dry and corporate. A far cry from what's needed on the ground.

Another finding is that half of all business leaders recognize internal communication impacts the bottom line of their business, but will often cite a lack of resource, expertise and budget as reasons for failing to invest in it.

But is that a false perception? It seems that an internal communication plan or strategy as a 'thing' is seen as being complex and costly. I don't believe it has to be like that. I think it's often more to do with not knowing where or how to start.

If you're looking for something accessible and erring on the side of common sense rather than grandeur, the Tools of Engagement Framework could be just the thing you need to think more like a 'connector' than an information machine, and give you the practical means to put great comms into action.

Involving leadership

If you're reading this and you're not the 'big boss' or ultimate decision-maker, then it's going to be the size, structure and culture of your organization that guides you as to how to go about involving those at senior leadership or board level in any planned activity for improving internal comms. Levels of autonomy, trust and delegation are going to be different in every organization, as will be the types of individuals and characters involved.

There's growing evidence that leadership is getting on board with the realization that effective workplace communication is needed in every area of business.

The ITPR Internal Communication report 2022/23 shows 77% of businesses (with 100+ employees) say that while there's no lack of interest from leadership in wanting an internal comms strategy, the resourcing of it is seen as a barrier. Ironically at the same time, it reports that leaders see increasing value in internal comms, evidenced by numbers like these:

- 81% believe it be important to company culture;
- 88% see it linked to employee morale;
- 84% say it's important to employee wellbeing;
- 78% believe it affects organizational reputation; and
- 69% believe internal comms is important to business development.

Interesting isn't it? So where exactly does this leave you?

Waiting for the board or leadership team to take the initiative is certainly one option. Or you could pull information together to make a business case for an IC strategy using the good old ROI (return on investment) approach. In order to do that effectively though, you'd want to offer some proof (or at least convey a credible belief) that it's doable and worth investing in. Otherwise, it may go down as one of those 'important but not a priority' ideas that won't result in action any time soon. Meanwhile, you're left juggling, firefighting and dealing with all those communication related problems – no doubt staring at your keyboard hoping for inspiration to come your way.

Alternatively, you could take the initiative directly and simply make a start towards something better. If the goal is everyone pulling in the right direction to achieve business success through an already agreed overarching strategy (and why wouldn't it be?), then why not help create the circumstances to get there, gathering the proof as you go. It's an option that could serve you and those around you well. And, of course, is now a real, practical opportunity with *Refreshing Comms* in your hands.

The reality of poor communication

'The single biggest problem in communication is the illusion that it has taken place.' – George Bernard Shaw

Great quote. George was a good communicator. In a few words he's summed up the problem which I'd translate as: lazy communicators rely on assumptions.

Just assuming that people know and then understand what they need to know is not the way to get people's happy involvement. We all tend to dodge things we don't understand for risk of looking and feeling stupid. The fear of embarrassment is real, and in the worst of workplace cultures, is only a small mistake away. So, unless you make sure people really understand, you're unlikely to get the best from them.

The many costly outcomes of communication gone wrong can stem from just one fairly innocent thing that then has an unintentional ripple effect across the organization. Often in hindsight, it's something that could have been prevented or at least mitigated in the first place.

When workplace relationships get really bad, employers may bring in communication and relationship consultants – for instance when things have gotten a bit sticky in terms of churn rates, redundancies or staff burn out. But hindsight being a wonderful thing, far better to prevent as far as possible the swell of negativity in the first place.

It's the big-name corporations that tend to be the ones we see making the headlines with the exposure of badly thought out communication and behaviour towards their employees. And the irony is, they're the organizations with the money and resources to seek the expertise and advice on getting it right!

But similar issues can and do occur in smaller scale organizations, and though they may operate in a less global or public arena, they still run the risk of significant detrimental effects that cost time and money, cause talent to go elsewhere and damage reputation for the long term.

Here are a few common examples of poor communication practice.

No news is bad news

Infrequent or delayed communication from senior management or leadership can happen for several reasons: lack of progress (nothing to see here), not very good news, and even indecision. But people generally much prefer to be kept in the loop whatever the situation, even when the news is 'there is no news'. We know this from other aspects of our lives, and felt it acutely during the pandemic. The need for certainty is greater than the need to be 'protected'.

It's too complicated to explain

If there's complex change going on and plates spinning everywhere, people are going to notice that things are feeling less 'normal' than usual. If they're not being told why, the resulting rumours that end up filling the void can easily exacerbate an already challenging situation, spiralling a downturn in trust, morale and focus.

Thanks, but no thanks

Asking for employee feedback and not responding to it is at best rude(!) and at worst a good first step towards breaking relationships. If a suggestion or idea can't be acted on for whatever reason, it's important to explain why. That way, that particular communication loop has been closed and you can move on to a new one.

The biggest offender though is this – a point which I can't stress enough, hence no apologies for the megaphone bold type: **You CAN be informal and still be professional. So, ditch any corporate stuffiness that stops you from sounding human. You'll be more interesting to listen to and be taken even more seriously, trust me.** Thanks, I needed to get that off my chest.

If you're too rigid in your approach, you'll come across as uptight and lose the power to engage, influence and persuade.

Have you ever read something that you just know has been written by someone fresh from a typical management course? Dry, clinical and stale – more focused on sounding clever and authoritative than helpful. Or listened to a person who has just read (nay swallowed) a management book and regurgitated what they think their bosses want to hear and would be impressed by? I know I have. And before I've even rolled my eyes out loud, I've switched off – attention gone AWOL.

If you watch a good salesperson in action, they're warm, friendly, polite and persuasive as well as professional. And guess what? They sell!

Being more relatable in your internal comms comes down to – yes, you've guessed it – good writing. No matter how clever or innovative the business strategy or new initiative is, or how fancy the diagram, if it doesn't resonate at an individual (human) level then it's not going to have any effect other than shoulder shrugs and missed opportunities.

It may sound rather simplistic, that you can make a difference just through a more considered choice of words and tone, but how else do you start improving communication?

Being relatable with employees (in fact with all your stakeholders) flicks the green light for positive interactions and constructive connections. When people are naturally drawn to you, things start to become a lot easier. And your internal comms is the one tool that holds this unifying power.

Time to lighten up a bit.

Let's play 'Been There Bingo' and see what prizes you win. Mark off the squares that describe something you recognize as a match with your organization, then claim your numbered prize from the list.

(In case your biggest pain isn't here, feel free to fill in your own number 8)

Unlike real bingo there are no fun prizes for a full house or winning line here. And if you've marked off multiple matches, it wouldn't be a surprise to find that your days involve a lot of firefighting, you have an overstretched HR department plus a business not fulfilling either its commercial or operational potential.

However, the good news is that any match at all is an opportunity disguised as a problem. So don't be disillusioned just yet!

If you have no matches – then whoopee! Put this book down, you don't need it. But in the interests of helping others, please pass it on or recommend it to someone else who could be scoring high on 'Been There Bingo'.

What the world is telling us

In this section we're going to leave your organization behind for a moment to touch on the big conversations going on in the wider business world right now. You'll see that it's employee engagement and communication that hold much of the solution to the suite of problems troubling organizations across all industries and sectors. Let's take a look at some of the hot topics.

Employee retention

The events and outcomes of the COVID-19 pandemic highlighted and then magnified what's really important to us, to such an extent that we've started to rethink our relationships with work. Less willing to put up with employers, workplaces and attitudes that no longer fit with our values or meet our needs (practical, emotional or psychological), we're getting more choosy.

Talk to any employer and at some point the issue of employee retention will crop up as an expensive headache. Across HR and recruitment agencies, it's becoming a conundrum, playing out through difficult negotiations and counteroffers, where employers battle each other for talent in a costly and rather unsavoury salary and benefits bid war.

The 'Great Resignation' and 'quiet quitting'

The Great Resignation describes the significant trend of choosing to resign or change employer because of dissatisfaction, largely attributed to the work and life changes, and subsequent shifts in priorities triggered by the pandemic. 'Quiet quitting' refers to employees who put no more effort into their jobs than absolutely necessary as a 'silent' way to voice discontent – a less aggressive term than its industrial predecessor 'work to rule' but just as unhelpful. Both of these issues have costly repercussions, not least with retention and productivity. And quiet quitters are not going to be enjoying the situation either. It's hard to get a sense of enjoyment or satisfaction from a job when you're consciously trying to hold yourself back.

Employer reputation

Publicly too, employers find themselves being scrutinized as people share experiences and opinions about companies they've worked for. Online platforms (such as Glassdoor) where job seekers can get a peek at what others are saying, are encouraging reviews and ratings that can influence people's decisions directly – especially if they're weighing up more than one vacancy or job offer.

Employee value proposition

An employee value proposition (EVP) describes what a particular employer stands for, what it requires of its staff and what it offers through benefits both financial and non-financial. Kind of like a promise between employer and employee, and also increasingly referred to as 'the psychological contract', the EVP sets out what the company and its culture can offer the employee in exchange for their time, talent, skills and experience. Traditionally focused on attracting talent, there's a growing recognition of its impact on talent retention through improved career wellbeing. And many companies are now revisiting their whole offer to sharpen their advantage and strengthen their employer brand.

In fact, Gallagher's 2023 State of The Sector report found that 56% of employers have started to revisit their EVP. Importantly, this includes reviewing and improving the way the EVP is *communicated*, with the report showing that only half of employers rate employee understanding of compensation, rewards and benefits as good. And of course an improved offer doesn't just rely on higher salaries. After all, that's not always going to be realistic and at some point will reach its limit.

It's no secret that financial reward isn't always the top motivator – important though it is. Terms and conditions plus salary became the package of features that people were judging their next job move by. But now, along with the need for more flexibility and work-life balance, other factors are joining the decision-making equation.

It's these other factors which can, understandably, prove challenging for organizations to demonstrate with any real meaning, as they're not as easy to quantify or prove in one fell swoop. Take environmental, social and governance (ESG) policies for example. These take time to grow roots and bear fruit. Similarly, for diversity, equality and inclusion (DEI) to be fully embedded requires a genuine, well-considered and consistent approach that becomes the natural way of doing things. So, by virtue, all of these significant influencers need to be communicated and actioned continuously – not just announced once with a fanfare in an EVP statement.

HR leaders

In its report 'The Top 5 Priorities for HR Leaders in 2023' Gartner revealed the task ahead for HR leaders worldwide:

1. human-centric leadership;
2. change management;
3. employee experience;
4. recruiting and onboarding; and
5. securing future skills and talent.

All of these five priority areas have direct links with employee engagement, relationships and of course effective, meaningful and intentional communication.

HR professionals already have a huge and varied work remit, with the diversity of day-to-day demands and compliance. With the effects of higher employee expectations now adding to this, it's no stretch to say that effective and compelling internal communication is going to be absolutely fundamental in supporting HR in tackling such priorities.

The economy

Finally, however much we might want to focus on the more positive things in life, economic uncertainty is undeniable right now, both for individuals because of the cost of living, and for businesses with budgets well and truly squeezed. So, here's a thought to chew over:

> Having a good employer–employee relationship is important even in the best of times. But especially so at a time when salaries are not keeping up with inflation, and when getting the most out of what you've already got is becoming so pivotal to keeping your business sustainable.

Across all the big conversations going on, not to mention the direction we're heading in, internal communication is your go-to tool, followed by action. Getting your comms in tune with what employees want and need from you and what you want and need from them is never going to be a waste of time!

Chapter 2

Reframing the workplace

The *real* narrative

It can be a tricky thing to understand and get to grips with – the workplace. Full of more characters, mystery and sub-plots than an Agatha Christie novel it can be a real head-spinner at times.

To get a clearer picture of what you're dealing with, you need to know where to look and how to translate what you see and hear into a common language that everyone can understand. In this chapter we'll uncover what's really going on. It can be very revealing and make your job that bit easier, when you know what – or indeed who – is actually controlling the business story as it unfolds.

At surface level, if we look at what an organization is made up of, we'd probably say something like people, processes and equipment. But if you want to be a good communicator, it's much more helpful to think of an organization in terms of people, stories and relationships. This is where we find the real narrative.

Reframing the workplace like this puts you in a stronger and more enlightened position to understand how and why emotion has the ultimate control and that it's actually logic that has to run to keep up. Then you'll be wiser as to how to leverage this to get the buy-in you need.

Within this real narrative are feelings and emotions – the things that give us the sense of whether something is going to be good or bad for us. Logic comes second and is typically used to help us justify our emotional response which will in turn dictate our behaviour and actions.

For example, if a person feels uncertain or anxious about something, they're more likely to come up with lots of reasons for not going along with it. By doing so, they keep their 'world' small enough to avoid any potential failures and protect themselves from the risk of negative feelings such as disappointment, frustration or embarrassment. But if they feel confident and inspired by an idea they'll forgive any risks involved and take it in their stride.

Did you know you're in sales?

Did you? In fact, we're all in sales to some degree. From world leaders on the global stage to parents bringing up children at home, we create our own formula for persuading others to follow our cue by nudging them in the right direction with what we say and do to achieve the best outcomes. I like to call it invisible sales.

As customers, when we consciously choose to buy something, it doesn't happen by accident. We'll usually have been led through a thought process (thank you marketing) that guides us to our decision of whether to buy or not to buy. When the process we're led through is done well, it'll result in us saying 'yes' or at least 'maybe' rather than an initial 'no way José'. And far from being Machiavellian, it can be really helpful to be pointed in the right direction. It saves time, energy and headspace. Who wants to search high and low for something they need?

It just takes the right message delivered in the right way to make the connection.

Even as far back as the ancient Greeks, philosophers like Aristotle had already discovered the art of persuasion in communication. The basic formula went like this:

1. *Exordium* – The introduction, opening or hook.
2. *Narratio* – The context or background of the topic.
3. *Proposito* and *Partitio* – The claim/stance and the argument.
4. *Confirmatio* and/or *Refutatio* – Positive proofs and negative proofs of support.
5. *Peroratio* – The conclusion and call to action.

You'd be forgiven for thinking some of those words came straight from the world of a certain boy wizard, but if these steps look in any way familiar it's because they went on to evolve into other classic formulas used today such as:

AIDA (commonly used in marketing, advertising and sales)
Attention
Interest
Desire
Action

and

PAS (a staple technique used in copywriting)
Pain
Agitate
Solution

You can see how the fundamentals have stayed the same throughout history. That's because so have we as human beings!

Honesty and trust

Being wary and suspicious of salespeople is understandable because some sell disingenuously and are dishonest in their dealings. These shady characters will misuse these persuasion techniques to the extent that they cause distrust and leave people short changed in all sorts of ways.

When coming from a place of authenticity – a place of truth and genuine reason – these formulas are not manipulative or scheming. What's more, people will never do what they don't already have an underlying desire or motive to do. That's important to know. All you're doing is knocking on the right door and getting them to come out and play.

By having people's best interests in mind, the collective success of the organization largely takes care of itself. Through these established and proven formulas, you're presenting people with a favourable choice that's hard to argue with.

Of course, the solution must then be delivered. You can't be all talk and no action. But you can set and control the pace. And realistically, delivering solutions is never achieved overnight. So, tell them that. Position your comms to encourage action and focus on progress through realistic stepping stones rather than patronizing, sweeping promises. It's the easier and more believable door to push at, and it helps you start building that all important storyline which people can then see themselves a part of.

Recognizing employees as customers

When we think of sales and persuasion in business, we naturally think of customers. But here's a question: What's the difference between a customer and an employee? The answer? Not much!

Well, ok – one's on the outside and one's on the inside. One pays the business for something in return and the other gets paid *by* the business in return for their time, effort and skill. But apart from that they're the same and equal in their potential for creating a positive or negative effect on the business itself.

Flip your thinking

Just by replacing some words for others, you can start to get an understanding of what this means – that employees are indeed customers too.

Customer		Employee
Attraction	→	Recruitment
Attention	→	Engagement
Purchase	→	Buy-in
Customer service	→	Employee experience
Loyalty	→	Retention
Voice of the customer	→	Employee voice

You can probably think of even more correlations once you get into this chain of thought. But the point is, whether customer or employee, all individuals go through a similar process of thought, emotion and behaviour, which leads us nicely on to the fascinating and super important topic of motivations.

The curious thing about motivations

Motivating people to think and act in a certain way can be a royal pain. A tricky mix of art and science perhaps. And asking people to make even a small change – a step away from their norm – can turn a person into the most negative version of themselves.

Over the years, I've lost count of the times I'd hear 'Ah, we tried that kind of thing before but it didn't work so we'll not be trying it again' and 'Nah, that'll never work here, we're different you see' or worse 'What's the point? They [the bosses] will only change their minds again tomorrow and it'll be something else'.

I can honestly say that this kind of 'shutters-down' mindset was the most common type of blocker in every organization I visited where senior management were trying to get people on board with anything slightly new or different, let alone transformational.

So, when you're re-thinking the inner workings of the organization and looking at it from the people, story and relationship perspectives, it's useful to be aware of the two types of motivations you're dealing with – especially when 'why won't people just do what's needed?' is the burning question that's driving you nuts.

Extrinsic motivation

People driven by extrinsic motivation are looking for tangible external rewards such as public recognition, awards, status and money – something outwardly concrete that satisfies their deep need to be validated and appreciated by others.

Intrinsic motivation

Those driven by intrinsic motivation seek and gain satisfaction from doing things that align with their personal values and beliefs – such as learning, mastering something new or being part of something meaningful.

The caveat here is that we all carry *both* of these underlying motivations to varying degrees and dependent on the task. So how does knowing this help you with your internal comms?

Well, aiming to balance these two motivators will go a long way towards encouraging more of the desired behaviours of positive engagement and involvement. Communicating shared goals, using a common language and creating a sense of belonging coupled with rewards and recognition aligned with organizational values make the ideal recipe for people to feel connected, appreciated and purposeful.

In the world of branding, marketing and sales, there's a universally known and accepted behavioural fact which is that any person who buys any 'thing' (whether it's a service, product or even an idea or cause) will have at least one, if not more, emotional motivators driving their decision to buy or not to buy. Sparking our little mental pistons, it's these emotional nudges that ultimately lead us into choosing one thing over another.

If you transfer this plain truth into the workplace where the selling (and indeed marketing) of ideas, direction and requests to employees is a critical but typically unconscious part of every people manager's job day to day, you can see why motivations become an important consideration.

Pain or pleasure

Thinking about the last time you bought something, you'll have made the purchase for one of two reasons:

1. **Pain** – Either to solve or reduce a problem that was causing you some form of discomfort such as unease, worry, concern, fear, inability to relax, putting things off or avoiding things altogether; or

2. **Pleasure** – To gain some pleasure such as the feeling of being relaxed, entertained, comforted or treated to something special.

Both marketing and psychology agree that pain is the more powerful motivator that causes people to take action. That's because we're programmed more keenly to avoid pain than pursue pleasure. So while pleasure is all about a 'nice to have' benefit which feels good, pain stirs up unwelcome negative feelings that add urgency to the moment and lead to immediate thoughts of 'I need to get rid of this, it doesn't feel so good'. And, of course, it's also true that many times when we think we're buying for pleasure, we're actually attempting to avoid or numb the pain we're feeling. I think we've all been there!

In summary then, the number one way to persuade, convince, coax or influence a person, whether they're a potential customer or an employee, is to roll up your sleeves (metaphorically speaking) and dig a little bit deeper to understand their pain points.

If all this talk of pain sounds a bit heavy and glum, remember that this isn't about focusing on the negative. It's ultimately entirely the opposite. If there's no pain, then there's no solution to spark people's interest. So, follow the pain and discomfort and it'll lead you more directly to the best resolution.

But what exactly do we mean by pain in the workplace?

Well, we're talking about those everyday niggles that hack people off but become grudgingly accepted as 'the nature of the beast'. You know, the things that annoy and frustrate the hell out of us but we believe we have to put up with because 'it's just the way things are around here.' Or because it's such a simple, mundane thing to put right it's not seen as worth 'my' time when there are more complicated things needing attention. Or you might just assume (hope) someone else with more time will do it. Crazy I know but we're all guilty.

The things that grind people's gears don't have to be particularly big or newsworthy. On the contrary, more often it's those small, otherwise seemingly insignificant things that keep occurring with almost predictable frequency. Take the damn photocopier for example, it keeps jamming. It holds people up. It's eaten the report. But who's fault is it? The person trying to use it incorrectly? The office manager? HR?!! You'd be surprised at where the blame can be directed.

So, how can you use pain to your advantage?

Gain from pain

If you're looking for simple ways to start proving (and communicating) that you're serious about making the workplace as good as it can be, you need to find and consider those pains from the employees' perspective by asking what they are, if they're not already known or obvious to you. Depending on what's feasible, tell people what's getting sorted with logical priority, get it done and let it be known. Even one small pain solved is more trust built, and surprisingly can often be done with minimal or no cost a lot of the time. The cost of not tackling them however, well, that's another story.

I'd just like to add a friendly warning here from my own early experience which is: DO NOT ask this pain question in a broad sense. You'll end up getting more than you bargained for. You're not going to be much help if you're drowning in a tsunami of random issues, troubles and coloured opinions covering everything from people, to processes to the meaning of life! Yes, that happened to me. Instead, give some definition or scope to the kind of *outcomes* you're looking to achieve from making improvements to help people be able to point to specific, relevant problems.

Granted, some pains will be easier to resolve than others, but by starting with those quicker wins that take little effort and resource but make something tangibly better, you're selling the right message and delivering the goods as proof to reinforce your intentions and keep them engaged.

Convenience sells

I don't know about you, but I'm a sucker for being sold convenience. If something can genuinely make my life easier, I'm in! So as a result there's usually no hard sell involved. How convenient!

Over the past few years, convenience, as a mighty motivator, has become a standout customer-experience strategy – helping some businesses leave competitors behind with simple tweaks to the way things are done which result in simplifying customers' lives. There are many stats (conveniently) that evidence this including these: 75% of customers would switch companies if they found a competitor was more convenient to do business with, and 70% would be willing to pay more for that convenience (Shep Hyken 2022).

If you flip your thinking on this, taking in its significance for changing behaviours, you can see how creating a better employee experience using convenience as a motivator can result in people willing to buy-in and *do* more. It just needs a bit of creative thinking and employee perspective.

The three main areas of employee experience can be broadly described as physical space, technology and culture, and all need the same level of thought and attention. Convenience plays into all of these in different ways, facilitating a better experience so people can do their best work. For example:

- Physical space: a well organized workspace with clear procedures.
- Technology: accessible, fit for purpose solutions.
- Culture: clarity of values and consistency in word and action.

Just like customers, employees enjoy having convenience in their personal lives, so the expectation and desire for experiencing the same kind of advantages at work is an opportunity that would be well considered by any discerning employer.

Conveying convenience through your communications, and demonstrating it in practice across these three main areas of employee experience, is a way to not only answer the 'what's in it for me?' question but to lighten the mental load and at the same time release more of that valuable focused energy on the right things.

The transaction

Life overall is a game of give and take. There's always a transaction going on somewhere – an exchange of one thing for another.

In the world of business, we all instinctively know how marketing works. The proven way to a customer's heart, and consequently their purse or wallet, is to offer them what they need at the right time, at the right price. In order to receive whatever it is, there's a transaction to be had. And with a customer, it's usually a swap involving money.

But with employees of course, it's different. Because the exchange isn't an immediate one, and is often less tangible. The 'pain' to be tackled or need to be satisfied may be here and now, but the solution could still be way up ahead – even for those who can 'see' it. This then is going to require a certain level of believability, consistency and reassurance in your comms (your selling technique) to keep the deal on track.

Getting more out of what you've already got

The biggest bang for your buck will always come from your existing workforce, the people you see every day. Let's call it your critical mass. This is where the latent potential of the business really sits in wait. Not tapping into this is the biggest missed opportunity of all, and will inadvertently keep people habitually operating at 40 miles an hour, even though there's significantly more horsepower under the bonnet. Never getting up to the speed they're capable of not only does your employees an injustice, but it's pretty rubbish for the business as well.

And by speed, I'm not referring merely to physical effort, but to the emotional energy stored in any individual that you can appeal to and bring to life when you know what makes them tick.

But hang on. Surely everyone is different? Well, yes it's true everyone is different with their own unique character, personality and background. However, there's one thing that we all have in common: we're human beings.

Now far from being a generalized, cop-out of a statement, this is a helpful thing to bear in mind, because as human beings we share some very specific traits.

What we all have in common

Ask anyone who studies the human psyche and they'll tell you that we're still very much primitive beings on many levels. For example, we all like to think that we make decisions and do things in a logical way, especially in our jobs. Wrong! Even if someone is known to be quite a practical, levelheaded and down-to-earth individual, their decisions and subsequent actions will have passed through an emotional filter. Appeal to the right emotions in the right way, and you're going to get the best response.

Take fairness for example. A sense of fairness is essential and as a manager and decision-maker in the organization, you show this through being reasonable and not letting personal beliefs bias your interactions with others. Importantly, you can also demonstrate fairness in action within your communications whenever you present a clear and sensibly balanced message.

Another thing we have in common is our deep-rooted desire and need for social connection through a sense of belonging. Internal comms is the perfect platform for fostering and demonstrating this to boost people's sense of purpose, improve their self-worth and increase their confidence. It's frequent, accessible and by and large free.

Emotional needs

You already know that your employees (your fellow human beings) want the same as you. That is:

- to feel valued;
- to feel respected;
- to know they are being kept informed;
- to experience opportunities;
- to feel they belong;
- to feel rewarded.

You'll also notice that there's nothing very tangible or easily quantifiable in that list. But the fact is we all recognize and relate to these very things. What's more, each 'want' on this not-to-be-underestimated list speaks to either feeling, believing or experiencing something. This tells us without a shadow of a doubt that emotions in the workplace are constantly in play.

Too touchy-feely? Nope.

Don't just take my word for it. Evidence abounds. For example, look at what Gallagher (one of the leading human capital consultant companies in the world) says about the kind of communication people are wanting in the workplace. Their State of The Sector 2022/2023 Internal Communication and Employee Experience Survey states:

> 'People want authenticity. Why do we keep serving them sanitized content? They're increasingly looking for genuine and transparent experiences – something that makes them feel good about their place of work… Communications lack personality and emotion. It's time to be braver.'

Good news – you're already halfway there

No really, you are. Let's start with the business basics. You already have:

- something to sell (goals, objectives and shared benefits);
- a marketplace (the workplace);
- a captive audience (employees);
- a platform (your role); and
- channels (emails, meetings, newsletters, the list goes on).

And most importantly, you have words and language at your disposal. Ok, I'm not trying to be facetious here, but you get my point? Sometimes we already have what it takes. All 'it' needs is a little organization and polishing.

Of course, your words need to be followed up with the appropriate and timely actions in order to be taken seriously and build trust. That goes without saying and it's a big part of your job. But I reckon, if you've made the decision to read this book, you already know this instinctively and want to get on and do it right. You're just looking for a way to start eating this particularly large elephant before it eats you. Well, I'm going to explain how you can start small and soon work your way around the whole big, wrinkly thing.

Chapter 3

The Tools of Engagement Framework

What it is and how it works

Now that we've reframed the workplace and have started to get a better understanding of people's motivations, it's time to introduce the Tools of Engagement Framework, which sits fittingly at the heart of the *Refreshing Comms* approach.

In this chapter we'll cover what the framework is, what it looks like and how its seven essential tools work together.

Each tool has its own dedicated chapter in which I'll explain in more detail the tool's importance and relevance to effective internal comms.

We'll also be using a helpful working example as a means of filling in the practical, customizable template step by step. At the end of this, you'll have everything you need to create and tailor your very own Tools of Engagement Framework.

In explaining these seven tools, you'll pick up important points about what influences people's behaviour, and how the Tools of Engagement Framework captures and applies this insight for everyone's benefit, including yours!

Shall we get on with it?

Here's what it looks like: A picture sitting within a frame.

So, let's break this down into its seven component parts. First, the frame.

The frame is made up of four core elements: Vision, Values, Employer Voice and Content Principles:

Vision – your vision statement.

Values – your organizational values.

Employer Voice – what you say and how you say it.

Content Principles – the all-important Rules of Engagement and Hallmarks of High Value Content for comms with impact.

As you'd expect, the frame and its four core tools are fixed, they don't change. The frame's job is to hold the picture in place, making sure the right things are always influencing what goes on inside the picture. That way everything can remain consistent and not be at risk of drifting from the organization's main aims.

Now for the picture inside the frame. This is made up of the three *variable* tools that are always subject to change and adjustments: Strategy, Communication Goals, and Themes and Relevance.

Strategy – your strategic drivers (commercial, operational and people objectives).

Communication Goals – the narrative and messaging that supports and explains the strategy.

Themes and Relevance – the common ground that provides the meaning and relevance of the messaging with your employee audience.

So, these three variables influence the detail of what your communication needs to reference in its content and what it needs to achieve through its effect, in order to create the right conditions for a positive response and outcome.

Now we need to make it super practical so you can actually use it. Anyone for a template?

The Tools of Engagement template

This template (or blank canvas to keep with the frame and picture theme) puts everything you need for reference all in one place. So, whenever you're discussing, planning or writing a communication, the right tools are there, helpfully staring you in the face!

Starting with a section for the ownership and purpose of the framework (i.e., the Terms of Reference) it sets out the seven tools: Vision, Values, Employer Voice, Content Principles, Strategy, Communication Goals, and Themes and Relevance.

So, for the first section:

Ownership

Decide who you're going to initially involve. The organization's direction will have been previously agreed at board/leadership level and set within the current business strategy, so you've already got your starting point there. It's just a matter of deciding which individuals have the most to give and to gain from their involvement.

It goes without saying that if you have a HR lead and an operations lead, their involvement and professional input is going to be a must. As key stakeholders with respective expertise and organizational knowledge they have a vested interest as well as an invaluable 'ear to the ground'.

TOOLS OF ENGAGEMENT CANVAS – BLANK

Company name:
Created: date
Last updated/reviewed: date
Next update/review due: date
Owner: lead name and position
Contributors: names and positions

Terms of Reference
(Purpose, Parameters, Updates, Review Schedule, etc)

Vision Statement	**Values**	**Employer Voice**

Content Principles

Audience (perspective)	Purpose (the point of the message)
Meaning (the benefits)	Proof (supporting evidence/ rationale)
Clarity (no ambiguity or jargon)	Value alignment (relatability to your core values)
Consistency (with other messaging)	What to expect (what they'll see/hear)
Round-off (the next step)	Call to action (what you want them to do)

Strategy Summary	Communication Goals	Themes	Connectors
Commercial			
People			
Other *(specify)*			

Eventually, and as a natural part of developing and embedding your internal comms further, other key individuals may go on to contribute and influence. It really depends on the size and structure of the organization. While too many cooks can spoil the alphabet soup, too narrow a viewpoint will limit potential. So, think about who the key people are and get them involved first to get the ball rolling.

Purpose – terms of reference

The rationale for improving IC in your organization and for using this particular approach should be set out within your Tools of Engagement Framework to provide clear and agreed terms of reference as to its purpose. For example, what it's to be used for, what its parameters of activity and influence are, and how it's to be used and maintained as a relevant, up to date resource.

A working example

For the purposes of filling in the working example as we go along, we're going to get to know and use a fictional company. So, before we crack on, let's meet our muse.

Welcome to Reed It and Weep Ltd

With 50 employees, Reed It and Weep Ltd has been around for about 12 years and does quite nicely but no cigar. Recently, as a result of the hit from the pandemic and an economic downturn, it's had to cut back on resources, isn't able to offer a pay rise anytime soon and has put in place a recruitment freeze.

The company has a mix of long-serving employees – with some due to retire soon – as well as a number of more recent recruits learning the ropes. Now under new management, things are getting shaken up a bit, so change is on the cards. Under pressure to improve the bottom line within a specific timeframe, the new MD and senior team are keen to get started.

They're also eager to keep hold of the knowledge, expertise and experience built-up in the business, retain the newbies they've already invested in, and want the company to become an attractive proposition for recruiting new additional talent and skills once some initial KPIs have been achieved.

They receive, not unexpectedly, a mixed response from staff when they announce their exciting plans, and are now working on different ways to get people on board.

But what a variety of people they have! They can see that, just like any other spectrum, there are varying degrees of employee engagement from one person to another.

So, to get a better understanding of what they're up against, let's meet a few of their employees who demonstrate quite nicely how engagement is a sliding scale of buy-in.

Highly engaged Helen

Enthusiastic in her work, she helps colleagues and always gives extra effort when needed. Helen is totally on board with the new plans and is keen to share her thoughts and ideas with management as she spots opportunities.

Non-engaged Nico

In his eighth year of employment, Nico is relatively satisfied with his job but doesn't really feel a connection to, or have loyalty for, the company. Being non-engaged he's developed a 9-5 attitude and if he doesn't get a good vibe with the new plans, he'll consider accepting a different job elsewhere.

Disengaged Drew

Drew is not happy. Having felt ignored when the others were in charge, now these guys are coming in to probably make things worse. Drew has no qualms about complaining to colleagues, and quite possibly customers too, so not exactly great for the morale of others either. Likely looking for a new job while waiting to have their point proved, Drew could be a bit of a loose cannon.

Turns out there are more Nico's than there are Helens or Drews. That's not too bad. Nico's are open-minded and can be swayed one way or the other depending on their experience of what comes next, so there's heaps of opportunity there to garner some allies. The Helens are all for what's next, and willing to go along with it provided there are opportunities to be had. Their positivity could help swing others in the right direction. And the Drews will likely do one of three things: either resign and leave of their own accord quite quickly; be influenced positively to some degree by the words and actions of the new management team and stay for now to see how things pan out; or leave on a mutual agreement that they're no longer a good fit for the company moving forward. A kind of necessary sifting process.

The senior team knows that the highly engaged Helens will appreciate understanding the company vision and will be looking for evidence of opportunities for contribution and growth to continue feeling fulfilled and motivated.

And that the Nico's will be receptive to a level of comfort and certainty provided by clear, consistent information that joins the dots and aligns purpose, meaning and values they can connect with.

Acknowledging that the disengaged Drews want to feel more in control and able to work things out for themselves, they need to make sure that communication is able to satisfy questions and quash rumours.

Finally, to make sure every employee knows they're valued and their opinions respected, they plan to build manageable feedback loops into the plan for helpful two-way communication.

Though Reed It and Weep Ltd is purely hypothetical, the types of scenarios and employee issues are very typical here in the real world. In fact, you may well have recognized Helen, Nico or Drew as someone you know!

Essentially the senior team needs to create a communication plan that has wide appeal but also directly addresses a range of basic needs within the content of the messaging – oh, and it's got to make sure those business goals get sorted. Sound familiar?

Building their Tools of Engagement Framework

The first thing they need to do is add in their terms of reference, so they're clear on what this document is and isn't, so let's kick-off the working example.

TOOLS OF ENGAGEMENT FRAMEWORK

Company name: Reed It and Weep Ltd
Created: 01.06.2024
Last updated/reviewed: 01.06.2024
Next formal review: 01.12.2024
Owner: M. Simpson, MD
Contributors: V. Lyons, HR; P. Khalid, Operations; N. Lee, Office Manager

---

Terms of Reference:
(Purpose, Parameters, Updates, Review Schedule, etc

- To guide the effective planning, writing, delivery and review of the company's internal communications.

- Used alongside current organizational strategy, the framework does not replace or alter any aspects of strategic direction already set, but will support and drive all related organizational goals and objectives.

- It will be updated in line with, and at the same time as, any strategic changes and reviewed regularly as an agenda item via the senior management monthly meetings.

- A formal review of this document will take place every six months.

- Feedback and interaction from employees will be gathered continuously using 'calls to action' within message content. Success will be evaluated via this on-going feedback together with the organization's current annual employee survey for gathering a mix of qualitative and quantitative data.

Now it's time to move on to each of the seven framework tools, starting with Vision. And we'll also dive deeper into the rationale behind the whole *Refreshing Comms* approach.

Chapter 4

Vision

Making your case

If you're a great communicator, the world's at your feet. In fact, it's hard to think of another skill that's more valuable. I mean the doors it opens, let alone the hearts and minds. But you need to get noticed first – you need to be relevant.

'Attention is the most valuable currency in business'
– Ben Parr, Entrepreneur

Great point. Getting people's attention is the start of making your case for the vision. It's the beginning of any powerful domino effect that, when properly organized, creates sufficient momentum to pretty much achieve anything.

Attention is what happens when somebody just 'gets' you. They've said something that resonates, rings a bell, stops you in your tracks, has you nodding 'I know, right?!' It gives you a feeling of being visible, understood and not alone in your experience.

Getting people's attention involves meeting the audience where *they* are, metaphorically speaking, rather than trying to pull them in towards you from your point of view. Communication that lets people know you appreciate and understand their position, gives you the opportunity to use that attention to move their thinking on to the wider perspective.

Giving people a larger sense of purpose

This chapter is all about the big picture – the vision, which is usually created at leadership level but sadly tends to stay there, rather than being shared on the ground with any meaning for employees. You need a way to translate the what, why, who, when, where and how by joining the dots so it all makes sense to those who aren't involved in setting the direction in the first place.

Better still, if you convey the vision as an unfolding 'story' that people can see themselves playing a role in, you're more likely to create the circumstances and environment where doing the right thing is easier. And you can focus people on the step-by-step journey and progress being made rather than just the destination, which can feel out of reach for many.

The IoIC IC Index 2023 report, looking at the importance of trusted sources of information, highlights the value of great communication from managers, and includes this quote worth noting from the Head of Internal Communications at Santander:

> 'The role the people manager plays on a daily basis, in creating context, alignment, pride and belief in the work of their teams and their connection to the business as a whole, can never be underestimated. For many employees, they (the managers) represent "the business", and it's incumbent on every business to equip them properly to undertake that role – giving them the content AND capabilities to have meaningful conversations with their people.'

When people, teams and departments can see and understand how they all fit together in achieving the organization's purpose, and that every single person has their part to play, the vision naturally becomes a more attractive and believable proposition. This more rounded and communally shared knowledge offers a more tangible connection between the here and now and the future ahead.

Vision of course needs to look beyond the organization itself because it never operates in isolation. There's an even bigger picture, a horizon that needs scanning and considering. It can be helpful for your employees to be aware of and understand these seemingly distanced but nevertheless intertwined factors that are going to matter.

I'm referring to customers, competitors and other stakeholders whose decisions and behaviours can have a good or bad effect on business. So, as part of the context you provide in your internal communications, give people a peek at the bigger view – what it is that customers are wanting, what the competition are doing and so on. After all it's no secret, information is out there for people to find quite easily so just be open. It not only demonstrates that you're on the ball and builds trust but also shows that you have a plan and, crucially, that you respect and value your employees enough to inform and involve them.

On that note, you also never know who in the organization might just have some brilliant idea or a spark of inspiration to share that could add value to what you're proposing to do. That would be good wouldn't it? Win-win.

By weaving the company vision into your comms strategy, you're putting yourself in the position of being able to share where you're going as an organization and how you plan to get there so you're more likely to have people focusing on the right things at the right time to make it happen.

Above all, treat the long-term vision as attainable. That doesn't mean you won't need to correct the course now and again, you undoubtedly will. But having your 'eye on the prize' at all times guides everyone, breeds confidence and allows them to keep taking the necessary steps to get there together.

In our working example, this is how the company sets out their vision:

Vision statement	Values	Employer Voice Guide
Working together as one team, we make and deliver the right products, with the best service and value for all our stakeholders so they too benefit from, and contribute to, our success.		

Linking words to actions

As we know, vision, mission and values are usually formalized as principles by being 'stated' i.e., written down somewhere. Some organizations will have all three of these statements, others one or two. But to actually have any meaning at all on a day-to-day basis, they need to be lived. If they're mostly unknown or ignored then they become pointless and risk giving people permission to take everything that comes from leaders and managers with the proverbial pinch of salt.

Also, new recruits are influenced very quickly not by what's stated, but by what they see and hear – the behaviours and attitudes of other people they come into contact with every day. And in order to fit in, especially during a probationary period, they'll tend to naturally do the easier and least likely to rock-the-boat thing by just going with the flow.

So, one of the goals of your internal comms is to help create and maintain alignment between what's stated and what's experienced, not just for existing employees but for those yet to join. And central to this is a conscious commitment to your stated vision and values.

A vision for change

John P. Kotter knew a thing or two about leading and managing change. In his *Harvard Business Review* article 'Leading Change: Why Transformation Efforts Fail' he explains why it's easy for a change initiative to get lost without a unified vision:

> 'In every successful transformation effort that I have seen, the guiding coalition develops a picture of the future that is relatively easy to communicate and appeals to customers, stockholders and employees.'

The fewer words you use to share your vision, the more likely you'll gain acceptance from your employees – interesting. So, here we are, back to communication and being more considered and skilful with words.

Because a vision statement describes the *future* it can be a tricky thing to write convincingly. I mean you're asking people to believe in something that doesn't exist yet.

So, here's a very important point. The vision must:

- be attainable; and
- have meaning for your employees.

As a vision statement pretty much underpins everything, it's worth spending time on. Is your current organization's vision still fit for purpose? Has it been reviewed recently? Do you even have one?

A 2022 survey by Gartner discovered that 52% of employees said the pandemic had made them question the purpose of their day-to-day job. A vision statement shapes and supports that purpose, making a strong case for a simple, well-articulated and genuine vision statement that people can see themselves part of.

Managing a negative response

Using your internal comms to keep employees engaged is going to help to minimize the almost inevitable negative response to change that happens before, during and sometimes even after an initiative.

It's not that people don't like to do new things or don't like change – we love it when it's our idea and we have that sense of being in the driver's seat. We'll have had time to weigh up the pros and cons, and having balanced the equation we go for it!

But when something is not our idea, that sense of happy participation and reassuring feeling of being in control isn't there. We don't know where the change will or could take us. Cue those emotions of fear, doubt and discomfort. Will I lose my job? Can I trust this company? I always said (insert name) looked shifty.

When first hearing news of changes ahead, thought impulses and emotions will tend to go into overdrive, which means people probably won't hear and take in most of the information at that moment in time. So, you have to expect some knee-jerk reactions. And there's an important point to make about this.

Your *written* IC holds the advantage of giving people the opportunity to read, digest and shape their own thoughts in their own time as they take in new information. An unrushed mind is a far better and more considered thinking machine than one that's under pressure.

Responses to change will always be varied depending on each person's perception of 'the great unknown'. These thoughts, as we've learned previously, are going to be based on people's past experiences and personal attitudes as they judge the situation through their own particular lens.

Another way to see the role of written communication is that your messages – or more to the point, the content within them – form the basis of employees' research before they act or make a decision. The quality of your messaging and the level of trust and engagement you build as a result is going to dictate how quickly and willingly your employees overcome any natural resistance to change, big or small. And when you think that change tends to be the constant state of play in any workplace, a good comms strategy is never going to be surplus to requirements.

The reality of negative emotions creates a need to process and hopefully tame them. For instance, people might have concerns about whether their experience or competencies are still going to be good enough. They may worry about having to use a new process or fear potential salary cuts or redundancies. Your comms can help provide some much-needed perspective.

Gartner found that 73% of employees affected by change reported moderate to high stress levels, which translated into a 5% reduction in their overall work performance. When you multiply that 5% accordingly across any size of workforce, it's going to be pretty significant. And that doesn't even include the knock-on effects on other people who end up being affected indirectly. The ripples of negative emotions, if not anticipated and addressed ahead, are going to be reduced productivity, low morale and less engagement, manifested in different ways.

Depending on the person, fear can show up as anger and hostility, mistrust or even depression and withdrawal. But if an employee has confidence in the organization, feels in the loop and part of it, their acceptance of change is going to be easier.

This is why the best thing an organization can have is a strong communication strategy to reassure, build trust and get people engaged and on board, especially when you don't have time to be going round talking to everyone on a daily basis. It's not just for the good times when there's happy news to share. Any organization trying to implement difficult change will soon find out how good (or not) its communication is.

Don't just take my word for it. Gartner's 2022 State of the Sector report found that 90% of organizations had planned change programmes for 2023. It went on to conclude that:

> 'Change communication is a fairly basic requirement for organizations of all sizes, not to mention a must-have skill for internal communicators — yet it remains a huge weakness across the board. While there are pockets of good practice, such as designing a long-term vision for change and creating a visual identity for change programs, a significant portion of organizations (58%) fail to articulate their **change narrative**, or understand its impact on different audiences. Neither do they maintain momentum with a calendar of scheduled communication activity.'

The change narrative. That's hugely important. If you don't set and manage the narrative, it'll start to improvise by itself (like a poorly directed actor going off script) and end up splintering into all sorts of different messages. Fortunately, with your Tools of Engagement guiding you, there'll be no worries there. The change narrative is the story you're telling, and we'll be looking more at narrative and storytelling later in the book.

You might be aware that poor communication is one of the main causes of change failure (Mckinsey) with 70% of all large-scale change initiatives not achieving their goals largely due to employee resistance and lack of intra-company collaboration – in other words, in the spirit of more plain speaking, because of people not working together. Showing that change communication is often ignored and only considered with hindsight (too late), the cost of failing to share a clear narrative has been high for many organizations. Probably because communication itself is taken for granted due to it being seen as a simple, everyday thing we do, so the focus, attention and resource gets put into the more complex, sophisticated and 'sexier' side of change and transformation.

While many organizations are only just realizing that the *content* of communications, and not just the act of communication itself, is the real game-changer, you're already getting ahead by reading this book, gaining insight and learning some simple but powerful techniques to apply in your comms. So read on!

Habits

Organizational change requires people not only to buy into the vision, but to be open to new ways of thinking and working in order to get there. And like all changes in life, that's going to require replacing old habits with new (and hopefully better) ones. That's why change can be so difficult. Like when you first commit to going to the gym three times a week, or eat less sugar, it's not easy to move on from what you've got comfortable with.

When you stop doing something you create a void – a free space where 'that something' used to happen. And if nothing steps in to fill that void straight away, it's more tempting to revert back to type and go back to filling it with the more familiar stuff.

So, replacing old habits with new ones is the way to go, but this is tough even for our own selves. Getting *other* people to develop new habits (not of their initial choosing) is a whole different level of persuasion that needs careful planning and handling. But the helpful thing is that because new habits are more appealing when they're associated with positive feelings and experiences, you can use that knowledge to your advantage.

By using internal comms to keep the vision in view and provide encouragement, you're going to help support people's efforts and first attempts at doing things differently. Keeping employees reassured and involved with 'the new way' through clarity, repetition and consistency is really worthwhile. We all want, and need, a reason to stay on track, and the content of your messaging can play a huge role in keeping the momentum going.

Price and promise – will it end in a happy ever after?

But, of course, it can be a long and sometimes bumpy road ahead. If you're asked to get stuck into change (and embrace a bit of uncertainty) for the greater good of the business, you need to have some degree of belief that it's going to be worth the effort. Because any change to the status quo requires a bit 'extra' from the people involved which can feel uncomfortable. That's quite understandable. Even for grown-ups!

The thing is, when multiple people in the workplace are being asked to do something different, that's an awful lot of individuals who need to be convinced enough not to hinder progress. So, where's their faith going to come from in terms of paying the price in order to keep to the vision?

Communication is going to help big time. Keeping the message clear, visible and present is going to reduce the risk of people getting twitchy. Fostering confidence and belief in a busy workplace where ideal scenarios aren't always possible is the smart thing to do. People have a habit of responding much better to being kept in the loop!

> It's not easy to pay the price if you can't see the promise.

You can't win 'em all

What if you don't sway everyone?

At this point, I'd like to assure you that yes, I am familiar with the real world and am not trying to paint a fanciful picture of 'communication utopia' where we all go skipping along, happily hand in hand together while the business makes lots of money. As we know, perfection doesn't exist – but better does, and that's always worth aiming for.

Despite efforts to convince them otherwise, there are some people who are not for turning. They're hard core and likely to have their own deep-rooted reasons for not wanting to 'get on the bus' you're driving. It's just a fact. Usually, the things that loom behind such embedded negative feelings and behaviours stem from sharp experience of being let down before.

Generally though, past failures, lack of trust, unpredictability, unhappy experiences (once bitten twice shy) and being asked to start moving away from all that's familiar and comfortable can all be validated, addressed and countered through your internal comms.

But don't worry if not every single person gets it. You don't need a unanimous vote to win an election, you just need a majority (as we know!). And, if the smallest of changes is meaningful then it's actually a big step.

Chapter 5

Values

Values are always going to play a part in business – they set the scene, the tone, the expectations and the outcomes. As part of the framework, they represent a tool with significant impact on workplace culture, and in this chapter we'll take a look at how they show up. But first we're going to get personal.

We need to talk about relationships

Outside of the workplace, we all know that relationships are the trickiest part of life. We have our own personal ones with friends, family and partners. And inside the workplace, different types of relationships also vie for our attention to varying degrees, but the same dynamics are in action.

Values when shared make for great relationships because they define how we treat other people and how we expect to be treated by them in return. We've already talked about all of the common traits we share as humans in terms of needs and motivations, and they're the same whatever the context. And broadly, the same goes for values.

In business, good customer relationship management is a strategic imperative. No customers, no sales, no money. The purpose of marketing and sales is to identify, engage, satisfy and retain customers. An obvious thing to point out perhaps, but sometimes the simplest things aren't necessarily given the attention they need or done well. A business might assume that their existing customers are happy, loyal and willing to keep buying but that's an incredibly naive assumption if the relationship isn't looked after – especially when competitors are also seeking their attention and are more than happy to take them away with a better experience.

Marketers continue to develop strategies for more effective customer relationship building and management, and they look to psychology to help them. Psychology studies the human mind through observation of behavioural and mental processes, including cognition, perception, attention and emotion.

You can see how such insight helps marketers to better understand buying behaviour and the values customers want to experience and come to expect.

This same kind of thinking has made its way into the workplace itself, applied in the development of people management strategies with the aim of improving employee relationships and productivity.

Swathes of research along with stimulating thought leadership is calling on companies to value and invest in their employees more. One such article voicing the need for a different approach is titled *Treating Employees Like Customers is the Best Retention Strategy* published by HR News (author, Ivan Harding). It says this:

'If businesses are going to stand out in an increasingly crowded landscape, they need to stop treating employees like a cog in the wheel and more like long-standing customers. This "customer retention" mindset puts a whole new lens on employee engagement and will help enlightened businesses win in the war for talent.'

More formally, the 2023 Columbia Business School study: *Are Customers 10x More Important to Firms than Employees?* talks of record numbers of employees leaving their jobs, and low levels of employee engagement resulting in the new phenomenon of quiet quitting we referred to earlier, which, it says, 'can significantly hurt a company's bottom line'. The study goes on to say:

'One reason for the growing dissatisfaction [of employees] might be that company priorities are disproportionately focused on the customer, while shortchanging the employees. Every company leader at every level, whether they manage two people or a team of 5,000, should consider how they think about customers and start applying that approach to how they treat employees.'

Agreed! Among its findings:

- Of the company transcripts studied, 92% mention customers while only 55% include any discussion on employees.
- Textbooks, academic journals and practitioner-oriented articles, which educate future business

leaders and inform current ones about strategy, are more focused on customers than employees.

This illuminating (though not that surprising) research is a great thing, because the more we understand how we operate as humans, the more we can create the right conditions for personal, professional and commercial progress.

Being authentic

This is a good place to talk about the importance of authenticity. Marketing and sales has, at times, earned itself a bad rep through a minority of mis-judged and dishonest campaigns that have exposed some companies as untrustworthy. Thanks to the growth of consumer (people) power and of course the lightning speed of social media, news of manipulative or disingenuous marketing practice is soon brought to our attention.

And it's the same in the workplace. People aren't stupid. None of us like to feel we're being schmoozed. Nor do we appreciate being patronized or kept in the dark. And we're keen to tell and warn others all about it if it happens to us.

Even a carefully thought out and well-planned business strategy or new initiative can lack credibility if it's not articulated and delivered genuinely. Over-egg it and people won't believe you. Underplay the effort it's going to take, and people switch off – preferring instead to freely exchange their own views amongst each other of what the *real* situation is.

And the resulting variety bag of mixed opinions can create a sticky mess that you just don't need.

So how do you come across as genuine by showing authenticity in your messaging? Better still, how do you make sure you *are* authentic? It comes down to values.

If you look at the purpose of internal communications, it's always been about communicating strategy first and then aligning this with a business's vision and purpose.

Then came along a rather seismic and completely unexpected shape-shifter in the form of a pandemic in 2020. The focus then turned to deploying tactics and adapting channels of communication to tackle hybrid working and crisis management. The thing I want to emphasize here is how important communication and the value of *trust* became during (and since) those times of uncertainty. Evidenced within Gallagher's 2023 State of the Sector Report, 74% of professionals interviewed now say that the purpose of internal communication is first and foremost to support culture and belonging.

This is starting to get attention in business, and people in the workplace want more of it. More values, more meaning. There's no going back.

Interesting times. Now that we're all 'experts' on the challenges the pandemic threw up and are moving on to pastures new, we're starting to see that while strategy, vision and purpose are still of course essential, there's a swelling and palpable need to create a sense of trust, authenticity and belonging in the workplace by shaping a culture that has soul as well as the means to make a healthy profit. And that takes good old-fashioned values.

Employer brand values

Values should be the cornerstones of any employer brand – setting the desired culture through what is and isn't acceptable.

The CIPD defines an employer brand as:

> 'A set of attributes and qualities, often intangible, that makes an organization distinctive, promises a particular kind of employment experience, and appeals to those people who will thrive and perform best in its culture.'

Similar to other definitions, it describes a collection of agreed or implied things that help shape and define the ideal version of a particular organization.

It also goes on to say:

> 'A strong employer brand helps organizations compete for the best talent and establish credibility. It should connect with an organization's values and must run consistently through its approach to people management.'

> 'Marketing professionals have developed techniques to help attract customers, communicate with them

effectively and maintain their loyalty to a consumer brand. Employer branding involves applying a similar approach to people management and describes how an organization markets what it has to offer to potential and existing employees.'

But an employer's brand isn't wholly self-owned. In reality, the brand is what employees say it is – or put it another way, what they say about the organization when the leaders and managers aren't in the room. It's a feeling, shaped by what the people who work there actually experience. And their perceptions and opinions carry weight.

That's because what they experience affects how they feel, and what they feel is going to directly influence what they think and talk about – inside and outside the workplace. And of course, people can vote with their feet too, which is what many employers are now dealing with – with increasing regularity. If your organization has never formally looked at articulating and establishing its own employer brand, no sweat, you now know you've got one anyway! But it needs to be one worth experiencing.

With your organizational values set out in your Tools of Engagement Framework, you can make sure these values are reflected in your internal comms and are serving to improve the employee experience and shape your employer brand.

In his book *The Brand Gap*, Marty Neumeier recommends providing everyone in a company with an organizational 'brandometer' – a durable set of ideas (values and principles) to be used as a compass that will always guide people to 'true north' when making decisions. Similarly, copywriters will refer to a set of brand guidelines for each client company. And you'll see that once you've completed your Tools of Engagement Framework, you're going to have yourself a highly valuable communication resource for establishing and embedding your own employer brand.

Here's how Reed It and Weep describe their values in the working example.

Vision statement	Values	Employer Voice Guide
Working together as one team, we make and deliver the right products, with the best service and value for all our stakeholders so they too benefit from, and contribute to, our success	• Integrity in all our interactions. • Collaboration, teamwork and knowledge sharing. • A safe and healthy workplace to enjoy. • Respectful of differences. • Lifelong learning.	

Aligning the internal and external brand

At some point, an organization should be looking to align its internal and external brand. And of course, these should be underpinned by the same values.

Naturally, there's significant effort and resource put into defining and presenting the *business* brand for the paying customers and clients. And that's great, it's how the sales happen.

But putting the same level of thought and attention into the employer brand has surely got to be important too. After all, two sides of the same coin, right?

Whereas marketing, sales and PR for instance will be among those teams or individuals responsible for how the external brand is communicated, it may be a different person or persons who look after the internal comms side of things. So, achieving alignment between what's being said and experienced inside and out is going to require a new level of collaboration.

If your organization already has a set of external brand guidelines, then make sure they feature in your Tools of Engagement Framework to harmonize with your internal comms.

Even if there are no immediate plans to formally align them both, factoring in your brand guidelines to your internal comms will help this future aspiration get off to a solid start, and pave the way for more collaborative thinking and communicating both inside and outside the business.

It's worth noting that those who are winning in the stakes of 'Employer of Choice' and 'Best Places to Work' are equally as conscientious of, and intentional with, their internal brand and their internal customers (their employees) as they are their external brand. And they know that internal communication is the golden thread that ties everyone and everything together in a favourable and sustainable way, especially during tough times.

Facts can become obsolete and plans can change, but values once acquired, never leave you.

Chapter 6

Employer voice

Why personality and tone of voice matter

Businesses that sound human are always going to be more appealing than those that don't. And this important little fact is the subject of this very chapter.

In the world of marketing and sales, the personality of a business shines through in its brand i.e., what it looks like, sounds like and feels like. If companies didn't bother to do this, then they'd all just be competing by selling commodities where the lowest cost producer is the only winner – a race to the bottom if you like.

So, a company's brand (it's personality) is actually a very real and valuable asset that makes it that bit different to any other company, and appealing to a particular audience. While it's pretty much an intangible thing (not something you can put in a box and give for Christmas) every successful brand out there has its own authentic and celebrated identity at its core – it's the thing that shows up all the time in how it makes people 'feel'.

As much as we love a shiny logo and a kick-ass colour scheme, good looks will only get a company so far. A recognizable personality and tone of voice will work much harder for you in terms of human connection than a logo, and allows you to be consistent in your messaging which in turn builds that magical multiplier of all things good – trust.

So, how do you go about defining your 'employer brand voice' and crucially, how can you inject personality into something as important as internal comms and still be taken seriously? Let's take a look.

Personality

The personality of an organization is formed by how it positions itself to connect with its audience. It's the combination of a certain set of characteristics and qualities that forms a distinctive identity. Just the same as how our own individual personalities make each of us unique.

In branding we often refer to 12 key personalities, known as brand archetypes. When you think about it, attributing something as fundamentally human and distinctive as personality to a business is rather smart as it makes an otherwise intangible entity more symbolic – something that can be liked, loved and admired. It connects people.

It was the noted psychologist Carl Jung who theorized that humans use symbolism to more easily understand complex concepts, and went on to call them archetypes.

'These [archetypes] are imprinted and hardwired into our psyches' – Carl Jung

Take a look at the table below which helps us symbolize abstract characteristics as personality types (people) we can readily recognize.

Personality (archetype)	Tone of voice
The Outlaw Disruptive, rebellious, desire for revolution	Bold, dares to challenge
The Lover Passionate, empathetic, indulgent	Sensual and persuasive
The Explorer Ambitious, fearless, daring	Aspirational, values freedom
The Ruler Refined, articulate, commanding	Powerful, shows expertise
The Magician Informed, transformational, creating the impossible	Imaginative and mystical
The Jester Fun, irreverent, in the moment	Playful and light-hearted
The Caregiver Reassuring, caring, warm	Compassionate and supportive
The Sage Intelligent, understanding, seeking information	Guiding and knowledgeable
The Hero Brave, empowered, accomplished	Candid and inspirational
The Everyman Approachable, authentic, accessible	Relatable and down-to-earth

Personality (archetype)	Tone of voice
The Creator Inspirational, innovative, original	Provocative and expressive
The Innocent Honest, simple, ethical	Wholesome and optimistic

It's unlikely that your organization will fall conveniently into one of these personality types – indeed brands are often a mix of two or three archetypes in varying percentages, and there are even subsets of these! But you can still use these main types to help you identify the elements of your employer voice, so you can use the full power of personality to produce more engaging and consistent comms.

Getting the tone right

You'll see from the table that each personality has its own natural, corresponding tone of voice that 'speaks' in a specific way that reflects its characteristics i.e., what the brand stands for.

For example, the Hero would say things like 'Where there's a will there's a way' – language that's inspiring, motivating and powerful.

If the Outlaw was saying the same thing, this sentiment would sound more like 'Rules are made to be broken' – a statement that's confident, bold and sassy.

Establishing an employer voice with personality is one of your key engagement tools for great communication, so it's time for the 'What's your type?' exercise!

Exercise: What's your type?

Get a few team members together and look at the 12 archetypes and their corresponding tone of voice. Do you recognize or relate to any? Do you even agree with each other and if not, what does that tell you? Pick out some of the most relevant descriptive characteristics and words for your organization – or add ones of your own that feel natural and reflective of what you're trying to achieve.

A visit to the working example shows that Reed It and Weep see their personality as a mix of Sage, Hero and Everyman with the odd sprinkling of Jester! So, this is how they've shown this in a practical sense as a guiding tool in their framework:

Vision statement	Values	Employer Voice Guide
Working together as one team, we make and deliver the right products, with the best service and value for all our stakeholders so they too benefit from, and contribute to, our success.	• Integrity in all our interactions. • Collaboration, teamwork and knowledge sharing. • A safe and healthy workplace to enjoy. • Respectful of differences. • Lifelong learning.	Professional and conversational. Understanding, supportive, inclusive. Friendly, encouraging, empowering. Lightly playful when appropriate.

It's all in the delivery

By delivery, I'm referring to tone – the *how* you say what you say.

It's an interesting fact that people will often refuse to accept an idea purely because of the tone of voice it's been delivered in. It can be surprisingly easy to turn people off inadvertently. You might be able to recall when this has happened to you – a person said something in a way that instantly got your heckles up. Or you thought you'd said something very innocent only to find you've just awakened Kraken.

Fancy a quick bit of science? I'll take that as a yes.

So, as humans, our primitive lizard brain is still very much alive and kicking. We might live more sophisticated lives now that we're no longer dwelling in caves or hunting down our bison breakfast, however, we're still wired the same.

When a message is delivered abruptly and with an unsympathetic tone, our amygdala (lizard brain) cries out 'Danger! Alert!' and we go on the defensive, becoming instantly suspicious. When we receive a message that has a friendly and understanding tone, our prefrontal cortex lights up like a Christmas tree – and it's this little guy that tells us what to think, feel, do, and decide. Turn him on, and you're on your way.

You may have noticed that the tone in which I've written this book aims to make it as effortless and engaging a read as possible, while still serving a serious purpose. I've used my personality and tone of voice a lot to shape the copy but without losing credibility and value (fingers crossed anyway!)

So, loosen up. Be brave. Break free of the usual stiff parameters. Enjoy using more colloquial language and be creative. Inspiration is everywhere. Find your authentic voice as an employer and add some natural warmth – and even touches of humour when it feels right – that people respond to so well. Your connection rate will soar.

When it's bad news

It's not always going to be good news that you'll be sharing. In such circumstances, should you alter your tone to the likes of Macbeth? No.

Any reality will inevitably include one or more elements of risk (uncertainty), otherwise nothing new is happening. And these elements aren't something to shy away from in your communications. Some of these risks or unknowns may be small and met with a shrug of the shoulders. Others might be more substantial and enough to cause a raised eyebrow. But it's always better to make some reference to them as long as they're being presented as an opportunity in an environment where it's ok to make mistakes if lessons are learned. When you do this your messaging stays constant, confident and positive.

What happens if the road to the promised land isn't straight? Well, it's never likely to be. The road will always have bumps, bends and even the odd unexpected cul-de-sac requiring a reverse manoeuvre. There's no long, easy Route 66 here. So understanding and pre-empting potential detours and communicating these openly but with confidence is going to be key to keeping people on board. That's going to require honesty, and in your role as manager, that means sometimes feeling vulnerable.

But that's ok. That's good. People want and trust honesty far more than they trust a too-good-to-be-true fairy story. So, whenever things don't go to plan, say so! But also say why and what's going to happen next that will help to restore balance. The worst thing you can do is try and use smoke and mirrors to mask the truth. All that trust you'll have built up will be knocked down. The reality is that being honest – and sometimes being vulnerable in that honesty – is a real connector with other people, provided you communicate and demonstrate accountability and a positive attitude in keeping to the vision while making any necessary corrections or adjustments along the way.

The following is a (slightly) modified but real-life example of a company announcement that demonstrates respect and understanding for its employees. Have a read and see what you think.

From time to time, we're presented with challenges. This is one of those times. And we want to be open in sharing what this means for you, the business and our customers, and most importantly what our plans are to reduce the impact, secure jobs and keep our vision attainable.

The unexpected non-renewal of our second largest contract will reduce our total sales by 20% from April. However, we've also made some great progress in building a share of the US market which is already helping to reduce the significance of this loss, and further opportunities here in the UK are gaining momentum. This is in no short measure due to your exceptional work ethos and collective commitment to the quality of the products and services we provide to our customers.

Please note that there is no requirement nor any plans for making redundancies at this time. And to actively prevent this as a potential outcome we've put an immediate temporary freeze on all planned recruitment for an initial nine months.

Meanwhile our leadership team is directing additional effort in supporting our sales team to establish new contracts swiftly and securely, and taking all steps possible to ensure we remain financially stable.

We hope for your patience, co-operation and your continued great work which are so important while we overcome this hurdle, and look forward to sharing good news of more progress with you very soon.

Rest assured that we'll be providing you with regular weekly updates, both written and in person, to keep you, our people, in the loop.

If you have any immediate questions, please do let your line manager know so we can address them as soon as possible.

Thank you.

By not shying away from the difficulties, and actually adding facts and numbers for transparency, the announcement achieves a high level of believability. Showing clear appreciation of the uncertainty for employees and addressing their inherent need to know as much as is possible and relevant, builds trust. The tone of voice is positive and solution-focused, adding some welcome reassurance. So, while the picture isn't ideal, the information being shared is certainly considerate of the audience's needs and feelings at that time.

Once you've established a more favourable way of communicating – one that factors in not just personality, but the basics of emotional need – you're going to find yourself having a far greater 'selling' effect on people, getting them to buy in to those short- and long-term goals, and most importantly helping you achieve them.

Even (and especially) when times get tough.

Sound check – how are you coming across?

If you want to know what you sound like in your internal comms, you need to do a bit of investigating.

This sound check exercise is going to help you get to grips with the current employer voice (personality and tone) being put out there, so you can spot if and where you're likely to have lost the audience's attention through messaging that's inflicted boredom, inconsistency or sheer confusion on people. Or conversely, at the end of this exercise you might be patting yourself on the back for a job well done! But you kind of need to do this exercise first to find out whether it's time to celebrate or not.

Exercise: Sound check

Take a random selection of communications (emails, newsletters, briefings, company announcements, etc) that have gone out to your staff over the last 6–12 months. Sit down and read them like you're an employee and it's the first time they've been put in front of you. What vibe do you get? Even better, invite a few employees (maybe new recruits too) to join in and give you their honest feedback on how they score on the personality and tone front.

At the same time, you can also look at them in chronological order to check if: they're consistent and evolve logically as a series of messages; that you've since followed up with relevant or promised actions; and if anything has inadvertently fallen below the radar along the way that needs bringing back to people's attention.

You might choose to do this review differently and more formally as part of a wider survey. The point is, whatever approach you use to take a fresh look at your internal comms, make sure you put yourself in the shoes of the audience first and foremost. After all, the whole point is to spot where and how improvements can be made. So, make sure any rose-tinted glasses are removed first!

You might be pleasantly surprised at what you find, or a bit disappointed – maybe a mix of both. Whatever you discover, it will be gold of the enlightening kind, and above all it'll give you the benchmark you need to get started on making some simple adjustments that will pay off.

Remember, moments of connection happen when a message comes across in a genuine and relatable tone, and it's pretty hard to write like that without sprinkling in some personality and human-ness!

So, here's to raising your message and finding your voice!

Chapter 7

Content principles

And now that you are finding your voice, you'll want to use it in the best possible way to achieve the outcomes you're after. This chapter is going to cover the all-important Content Principles: The Rules of Engagement and the Hallmarks of High-Value Content. Let me explain.

The Rules of Engagement

In the same way that personality and tone of voice are important to your internal comms, there are some other elements that carry equal weight in creating impact – I've called these, the Rules of Engagement.

Yes, your Tools of Engagement have Rules of Engagement! Think of these rules as your friendly (but firm) set of guiding principles. They'll help you keep everything in check which means you won't accidentally stray from producing great comms.

They may look short and sweet individually, but together they pack a punch.

Rule 1: Clarity

Every piece of communication must have clarity. Keep it simple, to the point and use language that people would actually use themselves, rather than stuffy corporate speak and claptrap jargon. While we're promoting clarity, let's also cover ambiguity here – a pet hate for anyone (unless you happen to be a cryptic crossword fan). We're all busy people. We don't want to be spending time and energy on trying to work out what something means. Ambiguity has no place in effective communication and only leads to a breakdown of trust which leaves people feeling threatened. That's why clarity is going to feature strongly in your new improved, refreshed comms.

Rule 2: Consistency

With each communication, you're basically telling bits of an ongoing story. So, messages that follow on from another need to be consistent and not conflict with or confuse what's been said before. Even if the storyline changes significantly, there'll be reasons why it's changed that you can refer to which will help explain the turn of events so people can keep up.

Rule 3: Purpose

If you're bothering to share something, there has to be a reason that you're telling people about it. Whether it's critical need-to-know information or a 'hey, you might be interested in this' kind of share, being clear on the purpose of the message shows you're respecting and valuing people's time, rather than wasting it. After all, you're paying for it.

Rule 4: Meaning

This is all about highlighting the meaningful benefits of what's being communicated – not just how something's going to benefit the business but what it means for the people in it as well, your employees. Rather than speaking to 'functions', you need to resonate with the people that make up those teams and departments.

If you think about it, when any of us are asked to take time to read something, and especially when it requires a response from us, we'll immediately start searching the content for one thing – meaning. What the information means to us and why.

Rule 5: Proof

In order to demonstrate you mean what you say, it's good to provide some proof. So, when something has been actioned, say so – or even better, show it. When progress is made (whether big or small), share freely. And if something hasn't gone to plan, be honest and tell people but provide your thoughts and plans for putting it right. Proof and transparency build trust.

These rules are not for breaking, otherwise you weaken your message. Thankfully, because these particular rules are rooted in common sense and decency, and are proven to work, they're easy to maintain.

The Hallmarks of High-Value Content

The most effective communications bear a number of hallmarks, that together deliver on engagement and persuasion:

- narrative (the story, the context);
- strategy (the rationale, the why); and
- compelling copy (the relatability and emotional pull).

The way to make sure you're hitting the sweet spot through consistent, high value content is to make sure you've stamped it with those hallmarks. And you can do this by factoring in the following.

Audience perspective

We all respond more positively when we can relate to both the subject and the person relaying it to us. But if at any point your communication starts to leave the audience behind, it can get a bit lonely.

It's worth bearing in mind something which has particular relevance to written comms.

First, as we read we think. And as we think we're asking questions in our heads (especially the more impatient or inquisitive ones among us). If these questions haven't been pre-empted and answered in the content, our attention starts to wane and is easily replaced with impatient confusion or frustration – or both! Like, what's the point of information if it raises more questions than it answers?

So, anticipating the most likely questions that may occur, and addressing them within the message content will help keep people focused. It's a bit like handling a potential objection in the sales process before it happens. It pays to consider what things might look like from where your employees are standing. What do they know already and what will they likely want to know next that's going to matter to them?

Value alignment

Make sure the content reflects or demonstrates at least one company value. It's not about 'stating' the value word for word (that would be a bit over the top), just a bit of subtle reference is sufficient. For example, if you're highlighting your diversity, equity and inclusion (DEI) values then support this with phrases such as 'we want to hear every point of view' or 'we're having a collective re-think as a company and are looking for diverse and creative ideas'.

Explaining the 'why'

No apologies for the length of this 'why' section – it's so important!

Your internal comms need to join the dots for people in order to have any context and meaning. It's important to link what you're saying to the bigger picture wherever possible. Whether it's company-wide, departmental or team goals you're talking about, help people understand by providing the why as well as the what. You don't need to provide detail necessarily, just the logical points that people can easily follow and fit into their understanding.

Sufficient context provides all the information needed to be able to understand something. For example, when you read a story or watch a film you learn from the very start about the names of the characters, when and where it's taking place and what the plot line is.

People need context just as much in the workplace. Providing the who, what, why, where, when and how, no matter how brief, will give people a far greater chance of: a) understanding; and b) buying into the idea. Leave one of those crucial elements out and you've given the go ahead for doubt to creep in.

As you set out to write your communication piece, make sure you're not making sweeping assumptions. It's worth bearing in mind that as the person composing the message, odds are that you're close to the subject you're talking about. You know it well – or at least you should! That's great from your perspective, but often when we're so close to something, we have a tendency to get a little complacent about the basic questions other people may have. Context is everything, and it's how we demonstrate logic alongside meaning without being patronizing.

Unintentionally communicating only from our own perspective is a common problem. 'I know what's going on in my head (I've been thinking about it for ages) so therefore when I write or talk about this people will know what I mean.' For example, have you ever started a conversation only for the person to look at you completely blank because you inadvertently started not at the beginning, but halfway through your thought when you decided to open your mouth and share it? Or maybe you've sent an email only to have to back track by filling in the gaps for the dearly confused.

Even if a person is articulate, they're not necessarily an effective communicator. It helps to some degree, but it's only one element of what's needed to get your message across well and as intended.

It's good to remember that context which includes the *why*, is the fastest and most considerate way to the best results.

Managing expectations

People will always appreciate a heads-up on what's next. So, use your message as an opportunity to set and manage expectations. For example, if an initiative is being rolled out, let people know what they can expect to see or hear in the coming weeks or months, and provide the timeframe that's being aimed for, if relevant. Or if there's some uncertainty ahead, be open about it but mindful that people will be looking for assurance of strong, positive leadership at the same time.

Call to action

What do you want people to do once they've read your message, if anything? We'll look at this more when we cover two-way communication later in the book, but for now, let's be clear that a call to action asks for a specific response such as giving feedback or indeed taking action on something. This is a great way to get people more involved and invested in the organization. So, wherever you spot an opportunity, use it. And if there's no discernible call to action (CTA), say so – don't leave them hanging!

The round-off

Rounding off a message well leaves a better impression than a weak trailing off or an abrupt end. You can always end a message by telling people what you'll be doing next and when, such as sending them a follow-up.

Overall, the main thing to avoid is vague messaging – it inhibits people. Having these content principles in your framework gives you a much greater chance of empowering them instead. Here they are together, captured in the working example.

Content principles	
Audience (perspective)	Purpose (the point of the message)
Meaning (benefits for the audience)	Proof (supporting evidence/ rationale)
Clarity (no ambiguity or jargon)	Value alignment
Consistency (with other messaging)	What to expect (what they'll see/hear)
Round-off (the next step)	Call to action (what you want them to do)

Chapter 8

Strategy

This is the biggie. Setting out what you're going to do and how you're going to do it, organizational strategy is where it's at. So, how do you get all that critical strategic stuff into your Tools of Engagement Framework? That's what we're going to look at now.

Depending on the size and complexity of your organization, you might have one fairly straightforward overall business strategy or perhaps a number of sub-strategies that link together, such as commercial, operational, people development and sustainability. And within these may be some finer detail, for example, DEI within your people development strategy and environmental, social and governance (ESG) in your sustainability plans.

Your Tools of Engagement can capture as much or as little detail as is necessary. As a minimum though, you want to include at least a summary of objectives for each distinct strategy covering the next 12–18 months.

You might have access to all this information, but it's at its most powerful when it's intelligently and intentionally organized for the purpose of amplifying and improving your internal communication. So, first things first.

Intelligent organizing

What and where is the information you need? For example, the internal documents setting out and influencing the organization's strategic direction such as business plans (general, departmental, short-term, long-term, SWOT, PESTLE); values, mission and vision statements; anything being used to guide workplace culture; any key plans for developing people, talent and skills; and any existing brand guidelines, of course.

It's quite common for this information to be stored 'all over the place' both literally and metaphorically! But well worth bringing it together if it isn't already.

You're also looking for any specific areas identified for improvement; anticipated changes on the horizon; people or culture issues identified and being addressed by HR; and ideas already being floated.

Bring all your key, influencing documents and information together in one place – and do it physically wherever possible. Commandeer a room and set them out on the biggest table you've got, hang things on the wall, get the flip charts out – do whatever you need to do to shine the light of day on all the key drivers you use to navigate the business and keep it pointing in the right direction.

Remember, you're creating version 1.0 of something that's designed to develop organically. It's intended to be reviewed, updated and built on as it becomes embedded. So don't aim for perfection – go with what matters right now.

And don't be tempted to speed through this in one day. Schedule some blocks of time in the diary for doing this, fiercely protect this time and get it done. You'll be glad you did.

The senior team at Reed It and Weep have now added their strategy into their framework. You'll see they've divided theirs into two areas, commercial and people.

Strategy	Communication goals	Themes	Relevance
Commercial **Growth and expansion:** Through best practice and innovation we'll expand our product and service offerings into new market segments and geographic regions.			
People **Investment in our employees' growth and development:** Provide support, learning, training and opportunities for all our people, nurturing an engaged, happy and productive workforce that contributes to the long-term success of the company.			

And with both strategies being interconnected, each influencing the other, they want to be able to convey this in their communications in a way that makes sense for everyone. That's when strategy takes on a whole new meaning and they can start to create a common bond.

> Being real and targeted with your communication isn't just a nice thing to do – it's a BIG strategic advantage for any business or organization serious about success.

The connective power of strategy

Strategy connects everything together, or at least it should! So being mindful of this in your communications is going to be key. After all, a full picture makes more sense and holds more interest than a few pieces of this and that here and there.

Which brings us on to the importance of a collaborative approach to your internal comms that I refer to as merging lanes.

'Stay in your lane' is one of those rather unhelpful terms that promotes, as a supposed advantage, focusing on what *you* do and not what others do, i.e., mind your own business and don't stray pal.

As an employer, it makes much more sense to be doing things that merge lanes instead. Otherwise, how can engagement, understanding and connection take place?

I point this out because if there's one thing that business improvement and culture change proves to you, it's that siloed thinking and working is not a recipe for success. It might be seen by some as the easiest way to go about your day at work, after all there's enough to do in your own job, never mind getting involved in other people's for goodness' sake. But it's hard to have a collective appreciation of the 'all of us' when people are wearing blinkers, and it certainly makes it impossible to have the 360 view that takes in the whole, big, beautiful picture.

Doing tasks that are seemingly unconnected to other parts of the organization keeps understanding and opportunities out of reach. When people, departments or functions only share information on a need-to-know basis, it's very limiting in every sense of the word. Through improved communication you can create an open and more inclusive environment that has a much better chance of delivering on values and goals for everyone's benefit.

Thinking about the typical set up in the workplace, you'll have different departments and functions each with their own roles and responsibilities. You might have employees and teams in different rooms, spread across floor levels – even sites and locations. And of course, there's hybrid working.

Though physical separation is often necessary and sensible, it can be a challenge in itself to get people to feel, think and behave like one big team. And to exacerbate this, if they're also looking, from their varied vantage points, at a fragmented picture of what's happening in the business, at best they'll just fill in the blanks themselves, or at worst see it as a complete mystery and decide they don't have the headspace to care.

Sadly, leading such separate lives with no shared direction isn't going to produce the best performance from anyone, least of all the business itself.

Connection starts and ends with communication. Whatever a person's role, they're part of a bigger machine. There'll be an upstream and a downstream of activity throughout the whole operation involving lots of other people doing their thing. Head down, busy doing what you need to do, it's hard to look up and see the common purpose that links all these separate parts of the process. It's easy to feel disconnected and consequently disengaged.

Using your internal comms to share insight and appreciation of the individual parts of the organization and the way in which they work together to produce a positive outcome, holds a lot of value. Encouraging interaction between different teams, recognizing efforts and celebrating progress as well as learning, gives people an idea of how they're doing and how the business is performing. What's more, it'll be easier to spot new opportunities to keep building this community connection. And adding a bit of fun into the mix is a great way to keep the momentum and traction going – it doesn't have to involve balloons and streamers, though having said that, why not?!

There are more benefits to this approach as well. Here are a few.

Culture

Ah, the 'c' word. We bang on about culture a lot in the workplace. But despite it having a dictionary definition, the reality of creating and sustaining a favourable one can be a bit like knitting fog.

Essentially, culture is defined as:

> 'The way of life, especially the general customs and beliefs, of a particular group of people at a particular time.'

or:

> 'The attitudes, behaviour, opinions, etc. of a particular group of people.'

So really, culture boils down to what's seen to be normal, how we do things around here without anyone batting an eyelid, the stuff we're comfortable with. Never underestimate the extent to which strategy influences and shapes culture by the extent to which it's explained and shared collectively and inclusively through your internal comms. Getting this right means you're in a far stronger and more advantageous position of being able to determine what the desired social norms are in your workplace.

Social norms

Social norms are basically the shortcuts we use that tell us how to behave in a particular environment or situation – the things we should and shouldn't do. In the previous traditional types of workplace hierarchies, there were many generally accepted social norms which were very limiting (not to mention nonsensical) such as:

- we don't question the boss because he/she/they have all the answers;
- we must stick to the original plan whatever happens;
- we will only get the job done through speed and efficiency; and
- we must work as hard as possible.

Thankfully this old set of social norms doesn't fit with today's workplace for many good reasons. Instead, we're now speaking up more, bringing ideas and trying new things. In other words, we're guided by a new set of more progressive and inclusive values.

When you're using internal comms to be more transparent about strategy and business goals, you're nurturing a culture of collaboration. The positive and progressive social norms become self-evident and part of the fabric of the whole organization. Through consistency of message, they'll naturally feature regularly in people's minds and eventually be less aspirational and more as standard. Sure, it doesn't happen overnight, but every little nuanced step adds to the difference.

Avoiding subcultures

While we aim to create a favourable and accepted culture, it's worth factoring in that certain groups of people may share situations, problems or experiences that are unique to them – and it's here where a subculture can form, creating its own narrative.

From my own experience, I've typically seen culture splits happen because: production believes that the sales department promises too much to customers; operations think HR is a waste of time; and the shopfloor roll their eyes at managers who might as well come from a different planet! And, of course, there are many more such divisive scenarios.

Different people with different skills fulfilling different roles is a great thing. Varying points of view can often be helpful for innovation, and in supporting diversity, equality and inclusion by challenging propositions or assumptions. But when it comes to harmony and order in the workplace, we need to be on the same team pulling in the same direction. That can be tricky to achieve when there are lots of people doing lots of different things in various parts of the organization. Which is why letting people know that they're part of the strategy (and why) is so important.

Communication that engages and connects sits squarely within all of this, so how do you go about writing comms that are going to resonate with everybody, whatever side they're supposedly on? For example, if a group of people are viewing a new initiative that they may feel puts them at an unfair disadvantage, the chances are there's going to be a lot of disagreement to deal with. Who's right and who's wrong?

Take a look at this top tip – I've seen this tactic work wonders at calming things down, repairing division and getting people focusing on what really matters.

When there's discourse that's disruptive rather than constructive, it's a good idea to separate fact from opinion. Facts are hard to argue with and serve to help settle down the background noise of conflicting opinion. A productive and inclusive way to bring things back to the facts and stop wasting time, is to do a bit of simple team problem-solving, and you'll be pleased to know that we'll cover precisely how to do this later in this chapter, so stay tuned.

Indicative of (but not exclusive to) manufacturing environments I witnessed many instances where disruptive sub-cultures had been allowed to form on the shopfloor – usually in the shape of one person becoming the unofficial voice and opinion of everyone else. Not because they knew more, and not necessarily because they had a higher position, but because they had a lot to say and by character were hard to ignore.

So, going back to the kind of communication that works for everyone through consistency, purpose and alignment, there needs to be one, unifying and trusted voice for clarity. Always aim to tie your messaging to shared values and collective goals. As one of your Tools of Engagement, strategy will help you do exactly this.

Quality over quantity in the battle for attention

You might be thinking, it's all very well to say keep communicating strategy to everyone, but there's a lot of it!

People will be drowning in the stuff! Well, it depends how you do it.

You'll be familiar with the popular phrase 'quality over quantity'. In the world of workplace communication it really does mean something. Too much information is just as bad as not enough. We can all relate to this on a daily basis. Emails, texts, phone messages, intranet platforms, meetings, social media, interruptions at our desk, TV, radio. It never stops, it's 24/7.

Mental overload is debilitating, and sets people up for making mistakes through distraction, confusion or sheer overwhelm. These are very negative emotions and don't serve any purpose in a healthy organization. Negative emotions follow through with negative behaviour such as apathy, withdrawal or even rebellion in varying degrees. Worse still, this can lead to work-related stress, anxiety and depression. To be prevented at all costs.

In a practical sense, when people have to sift through reams of stuff trying to find the bits they feel are relevant to them, important things can get lost in the battle for their attention. Too much in the way of messages, information and updates coming from different managers, departments and functions isn't only off-putting, it wastes time and becomes demotivating. Worst of all, if these messages are inconsistent with what's been said before, or communications from different departments and individuals actually contradict each other, it's pretty difficult for even the most engaged of employees not to lose interest and decide to dodge anything else that comes through.

So, we need to trim the fat so to speak. And once you've customized your own Tools of Engagement Framework, it's going to be much easier to do that.

Having a regular company newsletter can be really helpful for keeping people up to date. In the spirit of transparency and inclusion, it's always good to give everyone the choice and opportunity to read about other things happening elsewhere in the company. Inviting employees to contribute or including features such as a 'day in the life of' will hold a lot of social currency and give people a way of getting to know each other better. If you don't have a newsletter, you could always make that one of your communication goals.

Strategic problem-solving

In this section, we're going to look at why communication is almost always the root cause of problems in the workplace, why this creates unnecessary waste, and how a simple problem-solving tool can help you expose and put right these bugbears.

The blame game

When people arrive at work they all have very different days ahead of them as either an employee, manager or member of the leadership team. But the likelihood is that whatever their difference in role, they'll all want to have as smooth a day as possible so they can go home on time and without a thumping headache.

Although we don't plan to come into work to do a bad job, make mistakes in front of others, or say something that ends up in bad feelings, these things can and do happen with frequent regularity.

And while we can all appreciate that everyone's intentions are essentially good, nonetheless we'll often judge each other and swiftly point the finger elsewhere when things go belly up. Is it because we all inherently despise each other? Nope. Is it because a misunderstanding happened? Usually, yes!

When you bring to mind any of the things that have gone really well at work, you invariably think of those times and situations when people were in tune and pulled together to make the right things happen at the right time. It was good for you, good for them and good for the business. And no doubt, it felt kinda nice.

Then, in contrast, when you think about the headaches, frustrations, wasted time, effort, money-down-the-drain things that happen, you can bet your last Rolo that poor communication was at the root of it. I mean, we know this instinctively, right? (Other chocolate confectionery is available).

Playing the blame game can feel much easier in the short-term, but the problem with blame is that it never goes away. It just hangs around like a bad smell, and left ignored will only increase in potency!

Making sure that multiple individuals are able to carry out or contribute to tasks in a systematic, orderly and consistent way requires communication, usually given through written instructions. You can't run a business without processes, procedures and systems. They're all part of the mechanics of implementing strategy and doing stuff. Trouble is, they can be as much of a hindrance as a help.

Let's take a look at why.

Errors

As helpful as processes and procedures can be (though there's always room for improvement) if the purpose behind them is either unknown, not understood or ignored, you're going to get mistakes happening that will slow things down and work against the desired outcomes. And, of course, procedures are rarely designed for listening, so you've got to be proactive on being clear in the first place.

Assumptions

Too often people are asked to follow processes and systems that they don't really understand. They may well have been given the instructions as to the 'how', but in the absence of the *why* behind it, how likely is it that they'll be able to use it to the best of their ability, or have sufficient understanding to be able to spot problems? Without meaning, it's just another process with rules. Without the 'why', the instruction is weak.

Leading to limited understanding, the absence of the why lowers people's sights and expectations of what can be achieved. And at the same time, it says 'you're not important enough to be told why you're doing this' or 'we can't be bothered to tell you' and then we wonder why work becomes mechanical and people disengage. People inevitably end up focusing purely on the functional, task-based elements of the job, which naturally start to obscure and override the bigger, more important picture at play.

A process after all is the reason for doing something in a certain way. It isn't just a set of random rules. But without the rationale, that's just what a process appears to be, rules.

Providing what can be a very simple, but nonetheless empowering rationale not only makes sense, but it's also another great opportunity to communicate purpose. And it's also an opportunity to demonstrate your values – putting transparency and inclusivity into action by the very act of sharing the information. Feeling valued and respected in this way gives people a far higher chance of being engaged and performing at their best, which is going to make them feel good and you feel even better.

And remember the 'why' should never over complicate matters. So, the good thing is you don't need to dive into lots of tedious detail. As always, the simpler the explanation of the reason something is to be done in a certain way, the better for everyone.

 You can always use simple visuals or infographics to explain a process too. Considered an essential tool in the world of lean methodology, this is known as Visual Management – often described as the 'link between the data and the people'. Using visual cues and prompts like colour coding, it distils information down to its most basic form for at-a-glance, easy understanding. For example, a before and after photograph of an action, or green ticks and red crosses, can explain a lot with very few words.

Delivered but not received

It can be too easy to rely purely on the process and channels of communication in the workplace to get word out to people. These are important elements for sure, but without placing emphasis on the *content*, the messaging – no matter how many fast and furious communication channels you have in operation – can fall flat. And of course, delivered doesn't guarantee received and understood.

Over-reliance

More broadly speaking, just be aware of creating an over-reliance on rules and procedures per se. They can slowly strangle an organization, cutting off the air supply to common sense, creative thinking and the application of knowledge in new or original ways. These are the kind of great things you need not only for competitive advantage, but also for adding interest and variety into the employee experience. So, make sure there's room and opportunity for spotting ways to do things better for mutual benefit.

Waste

Generally speaking, waste describes any actions or effort that use up time, money and resource (not to mention patience and goodwill) without adding value or contributing to a positive outcome. And as sure as eggs is eggs, the root cause is inevitably traced back to a communication failure somewhere along the line.

Waste is an easy hole to fall into in any situation when you're not organized or purposeful. Sometimes the mere act of 'doing' seems like something productive is happening. People will hurry from one thing to another and have no time for a break, and certainly no time to stop and think for goodness' sake!

How many busy fools keep doing the same things while hoping for better outcomes. It could almost border on voyeurism watching them fail with depressing regularity. It's the same with busy but poor communicators. They make noise but nothing of value is heard. Because there is no plan or intention, just a tick off the list.

It's helpful to think of a problem as the gap between the reality of what people are experiencing now and what they actually really want or need. I always remember a manager telling me that whenever he heard someone at work let out an exasperated sigh, it meant that waste had just occurred. It got me thinking so I looked out for this phenomenon myself and guess what, turns out he was right. It's one of the reasons I'm such a fan of observation as a management tool. A picture paints a thousand words and all that.

Anyway, within that gap is a craving for better, which you can turn into a prime opportunity to make targeted and meaningful improvements. It shows you're listening and you care. And bonus, it makes life easier for everyone, so the business runs that bit smoother and more efficiently.

As a form of waste, poor communication is one with real knock-on effects. It smacks of not respecting peoples' time. Take a look at the scenario below as an example.

A manager is double-booked and asks Cath to help out by leading the meeting he feels is of lesser priority to him. It's a small team meeting, about an hour, so no biggie and Cath is just given a quick heads-up as to when and where the meeting is later that morning. With a very brief overview, no agenda, objectives or previous minutes, and no idea of who should be there, she ends up covering topics that are of no relevance to half the people there, and as such she can't answer most of their questions. An hour later the team walks out frustrated, disengaged and none the wiser. Cath meanwhile feels deflated and embarrassed which affects the rest of her week. Not only that, she takes those feelings home and ends up rowing with her other half.

Negative feelings aside, the unproductive paid time multiplied by x number of people for an hour was an unnecessary waste that you can directly put £ signs in front of. And then you can add to that the subsequent hour of everyone's time spent at the extra meetings and conversations the manager has to have when he gets back to put things right. In the end it was a good lesson learned but only after the costs had bolted.

While we're on the subject of waste, and as promised in the earlier top tip, we're going to look at a simple way of hunting it down and rooting it out! After all, if a problem isn't properly bottomed out, what's to stop it from happening again?

The '5 Whys' problem-solving method

In lean methodology, the aim is to find the 'one best way' to do something that everyone then adopts. This 'one best way' describes a process in which anything that doesn't add value but uses time, effort and resource, has been removed while any extra value is added (e.g., something to delight the customer rather than just meet their expectations). Once this one best way is agreed, it becomes the accepted, standardized procedure.

The '5 Whys' is a problem-solving method used in process improvement. You may be aware of it. It's essentially a lean tool used for finding where and why waste occurs so you can quickly target the solution and get rid of it once and for all. It's exceptionally good for hunting out sneaky 'hidden' waste that's less obvious to spot. Used as part of a change process, it can help make sure the workplace is fit for purpose in every sense. It's simple, practical and effective and a cornerstone of many highly successful businesses.

Now sure, this isn't a book about lean. There are experts for that – look them up! But in this section I want to show you how this problem-solving tool proves that communication is more often than not the root cause of workplace issues, both operational and human, and more importantly, how it can help.

So, back to the '5 Whys', also known as the 'toddler technique' (anyone with experience of little ones will immediately relate). A simple but highly effective improvement tool, it basically involves asking the question 'why' five times to get to the real root of a problem.

A really important feature of this technique is that it deals with facts, not opinions – and causes, not symptoms. Too often, the way an issue is tackled will be based on opinions. The trouble with opinions is, they are just opinions. And, usually, it's the person with the loudest voice or the highest rank who will have the last word. Even if a solution is felt intuitively, without facts you can end up treating the symptom and not the cause, a big waste of time and effort, and rather frustrating to boot.

Here's a couple of quick example scenarios where a problem has come to light that needs sorting out. The team gets together and tackles it by asking 'why?'.

Example 1

Problem: We've had a complaint from a key customer who didn't get their order.

Why didn't they receive their order?
Because it didn't get processed.

Why did this important order not get processed?
Because someone put it through on the old system instead of the new one.

Why did they use the wrong system?
Because they didn't know that the new system had gone live.

Why didn't they know?
Because they didn't read the email.

Why didn't they read the email?
Because they're skimming through or bulk deleting to try and keep on top things and it got missed.

So, an assumption had been made that everyone knew that the system had gone live because an email had been sent out. And deeper still, employees are receiving so many emails that it's causing operational bloopers.

Example 2

Problem: Erm, we don't seem to have the latest quarterly report ready for today's meeting.

Why isn't the report ready?
Because not all the data has been inputted.

Why hasn't it all been inputted?
Because there's a backlog.

Why is there a backlog?
Because the new software means it's taking longer to do.

Why is new software making the job take longer?
Because some of the data transfer wasn't compatible so it's now being inputted manually.

Why did we choose software that doesn't do the whole job?
Because the decision-making process had to be rushed so didn't involve all the right people.

Of course, you may get to the root cause of a problem in less than five whys or you may need a few more to keep digging, but you get the drift. The great thing about this simple and inclusive technique is that you and your team can apply it to drill down further into why and where communication isn't working, so corrective action is then much more obvious, easier and targeted.

Armed with this technique for getting to the nub of problems, you can then start putting things right rather than wasting even more time and resources on treating the symptoms – or worse, putting them off for another day that never arrives.

And just to add – if people generally seem to be finding it difficult to follow a process, then look at why. And if it makes sense to change it, do so. It means you're then managing by consent rather than instruction. And if you're looking for ways to build engagement, trust and cooperation, problem-solving holds rich opportunity.

> When people are part of the thinking and decision-making process, contributing and participating, they are far more likely to stand by the outcome and have a greater reason to do everything they can to make it work. They've been involved in, and so understand, the rationale and can 'own' it with more confidence. It's a much more favourable and enjoyable way to make improvements happen that also builds in resilience if things don't quite go to plan. And yet another bonus – team problem solving is a fantastic transferable skill to build into your workforce.

Chapter 9

Communication goals

Now that the key strategic drivers have been captured, it's time to look at the communication goals that are going to support implementation over the next 12–18 months.

These communication goals are going to help you focus on what you need people to know and why. Don't go into detail at this point, just root them out so they're visible.

The working example highlights *operational efficiency* as the communication goal relating to the company's commercial plans. And the communication goal to support their people strategy is *strengthening stakeholder relationships and alignment.*

Strategy summaries	Communication goals	Themes	Connectors
Commercial Growth and expansion: Through best practice and innovation we'll expand our product and service offerings	**Operational efficiency:** Continuously improve operational processes and systems to enhance efficiency, streamline workflows and optimize resource		

into new market segments and geographic regions.	allocation, ensuring timely delivery and cost-effectiveness.		
People Investment in our employees' growth and development: Provide support, learning, training and opportunities for all our people, nurturing an engaged, happy and productive workforce that directly contributes to the long-term success of the company.	**Strengthening stakeholder relationships and alignment:** Achieving greater employee involvement in improving customer experience and satisfaction through greater understanding of needs, new ideas and fresh opportunities.		

Success with these communication goals is going to require audience engagement, so let's look at what it takes to influence and sustain it.

How do you get people to say yes?

Employee engagement is pretty much a measure of a person's commitment, involvement and enthusiasm for their job and workplace. A passive individual isn't going to give any more than they have to, whereas an engaged person will get involved and help you make things happen.

An engaged employee knows how they fit into the organization's plans, and works towards achieving company goals in a spirit of cooperation and positivity. Who wouldn't want a business full of engaged, if not highly engaged people?

In the same way that customers buy for their own reasons not the seller's, your employees will engage with you for their own individual reasons and not just because you want them to.

Once people are thinking about saying yes, they'll be keen for more information to be able to justify their positive response. It's great when you do get people onboard, but you need to keep the engagement going. So even if initially it looks promising, it's not a case of job done just yet.

The stages of engagement

When a business is considering their customer audience so they can tailor their marketing approach and messaging appropriately, a key factor will be the 'buyer awareness' stage. These buyer stages represent a thought process, and can be likened to that of an employee embarking on a journey of engagement with an employer.

You'll probably be aware of the term 'customer lifetime value' (CLV) as a marketing concept, used to calculate the potential financial worth to the business of a loyal customer over a number of years. Achieving such loyalty involves understanding the customer mindset and using a number of marketing activities at different times. Starting with initial contact with potential customers, the aim is to move them through various relationship stages, with the goal of securing them as customers and then increasing their lifetime value by retaining their loyalty.

In the workplace, you can see the strong similarities with the process of employee engagement and loyalty from recruitment to onboarding and then retention. To help demonstrate this point, the following table unpicks these relationship stages and compares them:

Five stages of relationship building	With a customer	With an employee
1. Pre-relationship Engaging and influencing by →	Awareness/perception of company, brand and offerings. Demonstrating authenticity, expertise, social proof (testimonials from other customers) clarity of purpose, values and meeting/exceeding customer expectations.	Awareness/perception of company and its reputation as an employer. Demonstrating a good reputation both as a business and employer; having a clear identity and culture.
2. First touch-point Engaging and influencing by →	Targeting, understanding needs, showing the solution and providing a clear call to action.	Job advert, interview, match candidate with position. Alignment of values, purpose, pay and terms, i.e., the employer value proposition (EVP).

3. Making the sale Engaging and influencing by →	Providing a satisfying experience after-sales to encourage more sales from customer. Tracking, improving, developing trust and goodwill, communicating features, advantages and benefits monitoring.	Providing a satisfying onboarding experience and probationary period, and continuing the employment as per mutual expectations. Delivering on the EVP through continuous engagement, communication and support.
4. After-sales customer service and loyalty Engaging and influencing by →	Sustaining a mutually beneficial relationship. Converting one-time customers into loyal, repeat customers, anticipating and responding to evolving needs, deepening the relationship.	Enhancing the employer–employee relationship, creating a sense of belonging, providing opportunities for personal and professional growth. Interaction, two-way feedback, integrity, anticipating and responding to evolving needs.
5. Fan Engaging and influencing by →	Turning a loyal customer into a brand advocate to attract more customers. Providing opportunities for customer to promote brand and receive benefits in return.	Encouraging and enabling career advancement, a positive influence on colleagues and future employees. Providing opportunities to represent the company externally.

It would be very nice if the whole process of building such relationships was as straight-forward and linear as the table suggests, however, not recognizing these different stages and the opportunities they offer to enjoy good outcomes for both employer and employee, could lead to a messier and more costly journey – or one that's cut short with a swift goodbye. So being aware of the different stages of engagement and factoring this into your communications can help you do the right things at the right time.

Breaking off the engagement

At any stage of this relationship building process, changes can happen that present new challenges which in turn can threaten progress. What people initially based their 'yes' response on, the things that got them revved up and engaged, might now be looking and feeling different.

Maybe they were expecting a promotion, pay rise or opportunity that's now no longer possible. It might feel like one side of the partnership has reneged on a promise, and so the relationship takes a knock.

Change takes people through a series of emotional stages and it can feel like a loss. This is worth considering within the context of workplace communication and relationships.

This well-established model of the emotional effects of change, first developed by psychiatrist Elisabeth Kubler-Ross, shows the different stages we can experience:

1. **Awareness stage:** First reactions involving shock or surprise – and for some, panic.
2. **Denial stage:** Feeling resistant to change, heads in sand, disbelieving and scrambling for proof that it's all nonsense anyway.
3. **Frustration stage:** Accepting things are different but feeling hacked off or even angry.
4. **Depression stage:** Low mood, less inclined to be productive, feeling vulnerable and worried about not being good or competent enough anymore.
5. **Experimental stage:** First interactions with the changed situation, hesitantly dipping toes in the water to see what happens, hoping to find some meaning and reassurance.
6. **Decision stage:** Learning how to adapt, becoming more familiar, feeling more positive.
7. **Engagement stage:** More confident and now committed to making the change work by getting on with it.

As individuals, of course, people will find themselves at different stages at different times and for different lengths of time. Relapses and loops can even occur. But there are steps you can take to make sure your internal comms is doing its best at guiding and supporting people through change to keep the relationship in good shape.

FAB engagement

FAB is a technique used in copywriting to engage potential customers and lead them to a positive buying decision by pointing out the appeal of what's on offer, be it a product or service. It stands for:

Features – Advantages – Benefits

- A **Feature** is a fact that describes what a product or service is, has or does.
- An **Advantage** is what you can do with it and why it's needed.
- A **Benefit** is what the person gains from it on an individual, personal level and how their life gets better because of it.

The pulling power really lies in the benefits, as they dig much deeper into the 'what's in it for me' question.

As you can guess, bringing FAB into your internal comms is a good way to help you point out the rationale for why a particular change is a good thing – take a new computer system for example:

- Features: More automation, speed and remote access.
- Advantages: Less manual inputting, quicker to find information and can be accessed securely on your mobile devices.
- Benefits: Frees up your time to get other things done, no more frustration trying to find what you need and you can log in from anywhere, even from the convenience of home so you've got more control over your day (and you can be there to feed the cat).

The aim is to get people to re-think and judge something on the positives that are going to be worth the effort to accept or make the change. We like to arrive at a conclusion ourselves, so what better than to have information that naturally reassures us that there are real benefits involved.

And there are different types of benefits:

Functional: It works better.

Financial: You save or make money.

Experiential: How you *feel* when you experience the features, e.g., excited, happy, reassured, confident, organized, relieved.

Psychosocial: Even deeper than experiential, the psychosocial benefits describe how the purchase will make a person feel intrinsically good about themselves.

This last benefit is a really important one to take on board, because it's as true as the sky is blue that people will always, on some level or other, be buying a better version of themselves.

Have you noticed, for example, how a deodorant not only markets itself as a way of keeping fresh but is also selling a feeling of confidence and a way to attract romantic attention? Or that a cleaning product's fast-acting antibacterial features makes you a good parent as it frees up your time to do more fun stuff with your children who then grow up better human beings?

Being able to tap into people's already existing, underlying emotional needs or desires just as much as their practical ones, is the surest way to get a more positive response. And in the workplace, with a bit of creative thinking, you can frame communications in a way that helps employees picture themselves enjoying benefits while taking advantage of features. Try it!

Two-way communication

If we're talking about communication goals in this chapter, we've got to cover the importance of creating conversation from communication – otherwise whatever's said doesn't have a chance of making much of a difference.

Not surprisingly, two-way communication is considered as the best and most ethical practice by PR and comms professionals – recognized for its innate ability to engage and connect people. But, sadly, it's usually never achieved because of a messy mix of trust, hierarchical and practicality issues.

Around half of UK workers don't feel listened to by their employer, and don't feel their organizations are good at showing how any feedback they do give is used to inform the decisions and choices made by the company as a result (IoIC IC Index 2023).

These issues, of course, arise ultimately from the type of leadership style and culture in place, but that's a whole other book for a whole other time!

On this two-way topic, the UK CEO of Ipsos Karian and Box, Louise Breed had this to add to the IC Index 2023 report:

'Too often siloes exist across organizations when it comes to employee listening. The evidence here [in the report] suggests that less is more, and therefore a connected, aligned listening strategy to support strategic outcomes across the employee experience is critical for bringing together listening objectives for different teams, including IC, HR, ESG and inclusion. The impact of listening is significantly undermined when it's done for the sake of checking scores and progress and not with a clear purpose to drive change or input to decision making – what we call windscreen vs. rear-view mirror listening.'

Louise's emphasis on a 'connected, aligned listening strategy' that has a 'clear purpose to drive change' rather than checking scores is bang on. And proactive internal communication is the way to achieve this. If you want your comms to sound less like a one-way monologue and more like a good conversation, let's take a closer look at listening through feedback loops.

The importance of feedback loops

Because the best communication outcomes are achieved when room has been made for two-way interaction, feedback loops form part of your Tools of Engagement in the form of the call to action (CTA) which we touched on earlier in Chapter 7.

Part and parcel of creating interaction in marketing, feedback loops are great at prompting engagement, starting conversation and building customer trust and loyalty. The CTA is one that you'll see just about everywhere. Take a look at any good website or piece of marketing collateral and it will include at least one call to action, inviting the customer to do something, usually by clicking a button. Here are a couple of simple examples from two well-known big brands:

'Get the inside scoop' – Ben & Jerry's call to action encouraging customers to sign up to their newsletter.

'Lightbulb moment?' – Innocent Drinks' call to action inviting customers to submit good ideas.

The two motivate their audience in different ways. Ben & Jerry's plays on our need to be in the know, not miss out, and discover interesting things. Innocent taps into our need to be of value, be listened to and be appreciated. Though these examples use different motivators to achieve different things, both are strong in creating a sense of community and purpose.

By adding a relevant and engaging CTA to your communications, you automatically build in a feedback loop that intuitively encourages people to interact in a way that's good for them and good for the business, building a natural connection that's more sustainable as well as a progressive conversation.

When you're doing the right thing by means of two-way communication as a matter of course, it means you've always got your finger on the pulse. You're more aware of the current 'mood' and as such are in the position to pick up on and address niggles before they become unwieldy issues. Or you may gain some new insight that you can then use as an opportunity. You're also collating a lot of rich information organically that you can feed into, or review alongside, any formal employee surveys the organization may choose to carry out. I mean, why wait until an exit interview to ask a person's opinion? It's a bit late then.

To stress a point made earlier, another reason feedback loops are so important is that you can't assume as the sender that just because you've written something and sent it, that it's been read, understood and acted on. Better to know how your original message has been interpreted, and then you can use the feedback to make any helpful adjustments in the next round of communications. When people know they're being heard themselves, they'll be more likely to listen to you, and keep contributing. And bonus, feedback can often present you with opportunities to make some quick-wins that show that you've not only listened, but taken action.

The collective employee voice can be described as the sound of the organizational culture, and it has mass. When mass is travelling with momentum in the right direction, that's a great thing. But it's not so good when parts of it break away or wander off course because of misunderstanding. So, knowing what's being 'said' and 'felt' is going to help big time with positioning your message and making smart decisions.

Avoiding 'dud' feedback

To be of any value, feedback needs to be truthful. In face-to-face scenarios such as meetings where people can find themselves put on the spot when asked for their opinions, it's not unusual for lots of head nodding and concurring to happen in the room, only to be replaced with a rather different set of gestures or comments once out of earshot!

There's even a name for this. It's called the Hawthorne effect which describes the tendency for people to act differently in certain situations when they know someone's watching or listening. It's unfortunate in so many ways, and could suggest a culture that doesn't make people feel confident enough to disagree or have a different opinion. There are, however, a couple of ways to get round this and avoid getting dud feedback.

One is to instead (or in addition) look at things from the sidelines, catching things in their natural state of play. You'll need to be unobtrusive, and not obviously watching people as that's the whole point. I'm not suggesting you hide behind the rubber plant or earwig from inside the stationery cupboard, but you get the idea. A fitting quote that springs to mind is, 'You can observe a lot just by watching' (Yogi Berra, U.S. Baseball star). So true.

Another way to prevent 'false feedback' is to use the power of written communication. This works so well because: a) it gives people the time and space to digest the information or questions; b) allows them time to think about their response; and c) provides a process where giving feedback feels more comfortable.

Goodness. It's Chapter 10 already. Time to look at bringing the final tool of 'Themes and relevance' into play.

Chapter 10

Themes and relevance

It's this chapter that really homes in on joining the dots and doing the ultimate job of helping you connect people, purpose and strategy through feel-good internal comms.

With the communication goals in place in the framework, this is the way to now link everything together.

We're going to translate those communication goals into more precise and meaningful work topics that you can attribute projects, actions and specific messaging to. To do this we first break down each goal into relevant themes.

Themes

If we look at our working example, Reed It and Weep have translated their communication goals into themes.

Operational efficiency is going to involve the themes of:

- practical problem solving;
- reducing wasted time and effort; and
- creating room for new ideas.

Strengthening stakeholder relationships and alignment is going to focus on the themes of:

- collaborative projects;
- mapping the customer journey;
- new ideas; and
- skills training.

Using these themes, their internal comms can make the business's strategy and its goals more tangible, relatable and achievable.

Strategy summaries	Communication goals	Themes	Relevance
Commercial Growth and expansion: Through best practice and innovation we'll expand our product and service offerings into new market segments and geographic regions.	Operational efficiency: Continuously improve operational processes and systems to enhance efficiency, streamline workflows and optimize resource allocation, ensuring timely delivery and cost-effectiveness.	Practical problem solving. Reducing wasted time and effort. Creating room for new ideas.	
People Investment in our employees' growth and development: Provide support, learning, training and opportunities for all our	Strengthening stakeholder relationships and alignment: Achieving greater employee involvement in improving customer experience and satisfaction through greater	Collaborative projects between teams and departments. Getting people involved in mapping the customer journey to show the	

people, nurturing an engaged, happy and productive workforce that directly contributes to the long-term success of the company.	understanding of needs, new ideas and fresh opportunities.	importance of each team's contribution to the customers' overall experience. Generating ideas on getting to know our customers and they can get to know us. Skills training – interpersonal skills, avoiding conflict, managing difficult situations and delighting the customer.	

Identifying themes not only gives you a frame of reference to build your messaging around, it also gives you different angles to use to get the same points across. By doing this you're achieving a lot more 'reach' as you're not only strengthening your message, you're giving people helpful variations to understand the overall point being made.

You should find that each communication goal can be broken down into at least two or three themes. And in the spirit of being creative, it's a great excuse to go mad with colourful sticky notes so don't hold back!

Within these themes you'll have your own priorities as to what you need people to know, what you want them to do and why. Some things will be fairly general and others more specific.

Structuring your communication around themes makes it easier to plot and track what, when and how often you're talking about a particular subject. It also helps you balance the content you're sending out to make sure your audience receives the right breadth of knowledge and can enjoy some variety in their reading – as well as great substance, of course.

Just as importantly, you can also be confident that you're not neglecting any of the key areas that need to be kept visible, especially when you're particularly busy and there's more than one thing going on – like always!

Each theme holds rich potential as an opportunity for positive communication and you can really start to customize the content of your comms by drilling down to the specifics, unique to your organization and the outcomes it needs to achieve.

Relevance

Once you've found the themes, you then hit on what the relevance is to your employees. That means recognizing and highlighting the shared common ground and tapping into those basic needs and desires we covered earlier in the book that provide the necessary meaning and motivation. This has the added benefit of helping you pre-empt any questions of

'What's that got to do with me?' and 'Why should I care? I only work here'.

To find the common ground, you're looking for those win-wins where the benefit to the business can also be shown to have good outcomes for your employees. When you spot them, highlight them as having 'relevance'.

Having thought about this, the team at Reed It and Weep have identified several initial points of interest and benefit for their employees as you can see:

Strategy summaries	Communication goals	Themes	Relevance
Commercial Growth and expansion: Through best practice and innovation we'll expand our product and service offerings into new market segments and geographic regions.	Operational efficiency: Continuously improve operational processes and systems to enhance efficiency, streamline workflows and optimize resource allocation, ensuring timely delivery and cost-effectiveness.	Practical problem solving. Reducing wasted time and effort. Creating room for new ideas.	Opportunity to learn new transferable skills in work time. Less frustration and mistakes. Time and energy freed up for new ideas and better ways of working.

People	Strengthening	Collaborative	Improve your
Investment in our employees' growth and development: Provide support, learning, training and opportunities for all our people, nurturing an engaged, happy and productive workforce that directly contributes to the long-term success of the company.	stakeholder relationships and alignment: Achieving greater employee involvement in improving customer experience and satisfaction through greater understanding of needs, new ideas and fresh opportunities.	projects between teams and departments. Getting people involved in mapping the customer journey to show the importance of each team's contribution to the customers' overall experience. Generating ideas on getting to know our customers so they can get to know us. New skills training – interpersonal skills, avoiding conflict, managing difficult situations and delighting the customer.	understanding of how your individual role fits into the bigger picture and get to know people better. Help shape your team's role in getting great feedback from our customers. Opportunity to get creative and do something different. Learn how to get the best out of an interaction with a customer – and feel free to take these skills home and use them in your own relationships!

The six basic needs

For something to have personal relevance, it needs to hit home. We'll always prioritize taking notice of the things we know are going to affect us, good or bad. And as we know, to demonstrate relevance you need to be able to communicate meaning.

In Chapter 2 we looked at what we all have in common, from the need for feeling valued to the desire for a sense of belonging. Psychologists refer to six basic human needs which you'll be aware of if you're familiar with Maslow's hierarchy. But how do they relate to internal comms?

Well, these universally shared needs make us do crazy or great things whether we're at work, rest or play. So let's have a look at them from the workplace point of view:

Certainty and comfort

The extent of our own need for certainty and comfort defines how much risk we're willing to tolerate or emotionally bear. Knowing what's coming next gives us a nice feeling of being in control. Not being exposed to stress and anxiety of the unknown (risk) is a comfortable and favourable place to be. From comfort you can derive pleasure.

In the workplace, risks that threaten our comfort will usually stem from lack of information about what's happening. There may be rumour of potential job losses, a new leader taking charge or new technology being adopted. As a gut reaction, we generally anticipate the worst – a form of self-protection against the perceived folly of believing everything will be ok. Comfort on the other hand is clear and timely information, a supportive and approachable line manager and the opportunity to ask questions and share concerns.

Variety

To stop things from getting boring and samey, we all need a bit of something different to pep things up. Variety can be summed up as nice surprises you're happy to be presented with like choice, unexpected opportunities and new experiences.

Refreshing your internal comms to create more engagement and interest is a great (not to mention cost-effective) way to introduce a bit of variety that can be easily shared across the whole organization. Using your comms creatively and covering a range of different but interrelated topics is going to give you lots of content to keep people more engaged.

Significance

The need for feeling important, needed or special is a strong one for most of us. But, sadly, it's often only when we have a formal performance review that we might get to have this need met. The more consistent and genuine way to show people that they matter is through your everyday internal comms, or more specifically your Tools of Engagement. Whenever you apply the framework principles in your messaging, you're automatically addressing this need and more.

Love and connection

The big one. Love and connection are the things we desire the most in life, whether we realize it or not, or care to admit it.

In the workplace, these needs are met by being satisfied in our work and understanding our place in the bigger picture. Much of this has to do with having a purpose and enjoying meaningful relationships. Internal communication is going to play a huge role in this by setting the narrative that helps create these conditions for a sense of belonging.

Growth

Fundamental to life is the urge to grow and not stagnate. The fulfilment and satisfaction of having the opportunity to develop is not only healthy but drives us to do more, learn more and be more. A win-win for everyone.

In the workplace we want to feel we're in the right job and heading in the right direction. If your comms are meaningful, intentional and provide information that gives people useful knowledge and greater understanding, both professional and personal growth is not only enabled but will add to overall wellbeing.

Contribution

Referring to giving, the need to contribute is really the desire for meaning. Feeling part of a shared experience enhances both our personal and professional sense of purpose. Knowing our role and its value enhances our experience of giving time, energy and effort towards something worthwhile. Not just through the tasks we carry out, but also through contributing thoughts and ideas, so making good use of feedback loops and two-way communication will make sure people's desire to contribute is not only addressed but encouraged.

Being aware of these six basic needs and how they manifest in the workplace makes the case for better internal comms even stronger in the genuine pursuit of employee engagement, buy-in and satisfaction.

In an ideal world, making the workplace a good place to be is everyone's responsibility, employees included. But to start with, the direction has to come from the key communicators (the connectors).

And now, with a refreshing plan to help you scale the happy heights of communication success, anything is possible.

Chapter 11

Finalizing the framework

Great news! We've now covered all the elements of the Tools of Engagement Framework and learned a lot about what we all share, need and want as people.

So, for the first time, let's pull everything together and look at the full working example that Reed It and Weep have finalized.

TOOLS OF ENGAGEMENT FRAMEWORK

Company name: Reed It and Weep Ltd
Created: 01.06.2024
Last updated/reviewed: 01.06.2024
Next formal review: 01.12.2024
Owner: M. Simpson, MD
Contributors: V. Lyons, HR; P. Khalid, Operations; N. Lee, Office Manager

Terms of Reference:
(Purpose, Parameters, Updates, Review Schedule, etc)

- To guide the effective planning, writing, delivery and review of the company's internal communications.

- Used alongside current organizational strategy, the framework does not replace or alter any aspects of strategic direction already set, but will support and drive all related organizational goals and objectives.

- It will be updated in line with, and at the same time as, any strategic changes and reviewed regularly as an agenda item via the senior management monthly meetings.

- A formal review of this document will take place every six months.

- Feedback and interaction from employees will be gathered continuously using 'calls to action' within message content. Success will be evaluated via this on-going feedback together with the organization's current annual employee survey for gathering a mix of qualitative and quantitative data.

Vision statement	Values	Employer voice
Working together as one team, we make and deliver the right products, with the best service and value for all our stakeholders so they too benefit from, and contribute to, our success.	• Integrity in all our interactions. • Collaboration, teamwork and knowledge sharing. • A safe and healthy workplace to enjoy. • Respectful of differences. • Lifelong learning.	Professional and conversational. Understanding, supportive, inclusive. Friendly, encouraging, empowering. Lightly playful when appropriate.

Content principles

Audience (perspective)	Purpose (the point of the message)
Meaning (benefits for the audience)	Proof (supporting evidence/ rationale)
Clarity (no ambiguity or jargon)	Value alignment (relatability to your core values)
Consistency (with other messaging)	What to expect (what they'll see/ hear)
Round-off (the next step)	Call to action (what you want them to do)

Strategy	Communication goals	Themes	Relevance
Commercial Growth and expansion: Through best practice and innovation we'll expand our product and service offerings into new market segments and geographic regions.	**Operational efficiency:** Continuously improve operational processes and systems to enhance efficiency, streamline workflows and optimize resource allocation, ensuring timely delivery and cost-effectiveness.	Practical problem solving. Reducing wasted time and effort. Creating room for new ideas.	Opportunity to learn new transferable skills in work time. Less frustration and mistakes. Time and energy freed up for new ideas and better ways of working.
People Investment in our employees' growth and development: Provide support, learning, training and opportunities for all our people, nurturing an engaged, happy and productive workforce that contributes to the long-term success of the company.	**Strengthening stakeholder relationships and alignment:** Achieving greater employee involvement in improving customer experience and satisfaction through greater understanding of needs, new ideas and fresh opportunities.	Collaborative projects between teams and departments. Getting people involved in mapping the customer journey to show the importance of each team's contribution to the customers' overall experience. Generating ideas on getting to	Improve your understanding of how your individual role fits into the bigger picture and get to know people better. Help shape your team's role in getting great feedback from our customers. Opportunity to get creative and do something different.

		know our customers so they can get to know us. Skills training – interpersonal skills, avoiding conflict, managing difficult situations and delighting the customer.	Learn how to get the best out of an interaction with a customer – and feel free to take these skills home and use them in your own relationships!

They're now well-prepared to start introducing the new company strategy to their employees. With their communication goals identified and the ability to clearly show how these goals have meaning, relevance and benefits for their employees, they're ready to write their first communication.

As a practical way of categorizing and keeping track of all the communications they send out over time, they're going to use this 'message masterfile' for the writing and easy referencing of messages.

Each communication goal in the framework will have its own message masterfile for writing and keeping record of the series of related messages pertaining to that goal, all captured in the one document – helping them stay on point and be consistent, so the 'story' continues, trust builds and buy-in increases.

You'll see that it has a helpful checklist and references to guide the message content as you write.

Message masterfile

Employer Voice Guide – our style and tone of writing:	Communication goal:
Checklist • Targeted (the right audience) • Audience (their perspective) • Purpose (the point of the message) • Meaning (benefits for the audience) • Proof (supporting evidence/ rationale) • Clarity (no ambiguity or jargon) • Consistency (with previous/ other messaging) • What to expect (what they'll see/hear) • Call to action (what you want them to do) • Round-off (the next step)	**What the message is promoting and encouraging:** **Why this matters/is of benefit to our employees:**

Write message here
Header: Main text: Call to action:

Once written, each message can be sent out as normal with a quick copy and paste, and the original saved here in the masterfile.

So, let's look at this as a working example.

Reed It and Weep want to start communicating their goal of operational efficiency. They've composed their first message using the masterfile.

Guided by the checklist, they've made sure the rules and hallmarks of great comms are all there – and these have been highlighted for your reference in the written message using bold italics.

Employer Voice Guide – our style and tone of writing: • Professional • Conversational • Understanding, supportive, inclusive • Friendly, encouraging, empowering • Light-touch playful when appropriate	**Communication goal:** Operational efficiency
Checklist ☑ Targeted (the right audience) ☑ Audience (their perspective) ☑ Purpose (the point of the message)	**What the message is promoting and encouraging:** Practical problem solving Reducing wasted time and effort New ideas

☑ Meaning (benefits for the audience)	**Why this matters/is of benefit to our employees**
☑ Alignment with values	Less frustration and mistakes
☑ Proof (supporting evidence/rationale)	Opportunity to learn a new problem solving skill
☑ Clarity (no ambiguity or jargon)	Time and energy freed up for new ideas
☑ Consistency (with previous/other messaging)	
☑ What to expect (what they'll see/hear)	
☑ Call to action (what you want them to do)	
☑ Round-off (the next step)	

Content

Header: We need your lightbulbs!

Have you ever thought we could do something in a better way? Had one of those lightbulb moments?

With some practical problem-solving we can make small improvements with big impact. Making sure we have better processes, tools and support in place for every task means we can all do a good job together and go home less tired! So, we're asking for your help *(✓ purpose and meaning)*.

By joining in and sharing your thinking and ideas you'll be making a huge difference – with the bonus that you'll be learning a new, simple but highly transferable problem-solving method in the process to support your own professional development *(✓ alignment with values)*.

A total of 9hrs per week have already been saved in the warehouse with two small changes – the team feedback is that they're feeling less rushed and able to spend more time on planning which is working really well for them. We'd like everyone to have the same opportunity so you can experience the benefits and satisfaction *(✓ proof)*.

> You'll notice a focus over the next 12 months on making practical improvements wherever possible so we can truly fulfil our vision of being the trusted partner of choice for our customers. We're planning to recognize and celebrate your lightbulb moments with a party/get-together later in the year *(✓ what to expect)*.
>
> If you'd like to be part of a problem-solving team that gets rid of an annoying issue, and learn a new skill at the same time, or would like to be part of the party planning brigade later in the year, just complete and return the attached form before (date) *(✓ call to action)*.
>
> We'll update you on responses in two week's time before we start planning and announcing the first teams and improvement projects *(✓ round-off)*.
>
> Thank you in advance for your illuminating input!

Some messages will be appropriately short and sweet, and others more long-form like this one.

If you're feeling a bit overwhelmed when it comes to the writing stage, don't be. We've already established that perfect doesn't exist, but better does. And that's what you're doing – taking solid steps to putting better messages out there to greater effect.

 A good tip when you're getting started is to write with one person in mind who best represents your main audience. Remember we all want the same things so if you get it right for one person, you'll get it right for most.

So don't put it off any longer and do your best. You might even enjoy it!

'The secret of getting ahead is getting started.' – Mark Twain

Chapter 12

How to write like a pro

In this bonus chapter I'll be sharing some additional professional copywriting techniques used in persuasive messaging that you can factor into your *Refreshing Comms* for extra relatability.

And we're going to start with a good one.

Forget the rules

Whaat?! Forget what my English teacher Miss Whatsername taught me? Those immortal dos and don'ts etched on my brain? I can't do that!

Well, the good news is that yes you can. No disrespect to Miss Whatsername or any other English teachers, they're wonderful and have their job to do. And I'm not encouraging spelling mistakes either (that just won't do at all). I'm talking about relaxing those strict grammatical rules that make a piece of writing as stiff as a starched collar and just as comfortable.

If you're focusing too much on the technical dos and don'ts of sentence structure, then you're not going to be paying enough attention to the essence and intention of the message. So, I absolutely encourage you to use these tips and you'll soon see how, with practice and ease, you'll be happily no longer constrained by the writing police!

Make it conversational

Read this:

> 'Engineering is the practice of using natural science, mathematics and the scientific method to solve problems, increase efficiency and productivity, and improve systems. It offers a number of routes as a career choice.'

Now this:

> 'Engineering solves problems for people by using science and maths to improve systems. That way things can run more efficiently and productively. It's a fantastically rewarding career with lots of opportunities.'

Which was a better read for you? The second one? Yes, me too.

Conversational tone is an informal style of writing. Aiming for conversational means being more relaxed through word choice, sentence structure and other elements such as a bit of personality, to give the effect that you're a human being talking and not a 'business' reciting some information. When you get this right you build an authentic connection with your audience because they feel like they're reading something you've written especially for them.

Use sentence fragments

Breaking news: it's ok to start sentences with words such as 'and' or 'but' or 'because'. Doing this means you can use shorter sentences which are easier to read, so people don't have to stop mid-flow to mentally translate – a sure fire way for them to not only lose interest but lose the plot!

When you relax and write conversationally, you instantly become more relatable, engaging and far more likely to get and hold attention – nobody's going to be returning your message covered in red ink corrections (even Miss you know who).

Sentence length

Have you got rhythm? A key principle of professional copywriting is to use a variety of sentence lengths to avoid things getting monotonous for the reader. When we're talking about 'loosening up' in our comms, something that can often get overlooked is rhythm. A personable, appealing read has cadence – a natural rhythmic flow of words.

Now, back up the truck a minute. I realize you're not reading this book because you want to become the next poet laureate – you just want to get better results from better communication – so let's keep this really simple.

You can keep things interesting by creating rhythm using a mix of long, short and punchy sentences and blending them together in your message. This book offers a good example of doing just that. So right here, in your hands (or on your screen), are many examples of how it's done. You're welcome.

This also gives your words life and energy, making them more engaging to read. A handy benchmark is to read your copy out loud, and if you come up gasping for air, you know it's going to be a good idea to break it up a bit more!

Contractions

Another way to relax and loosen up your writing is to use contractions – mashing two words together to make them shorter, like we usually do in verbal conversations. You may do this already but if you don't, have a quick look at the difference it can make:

> We are planning a training day tomorrow. Do not forget to bring your laptops.

Or

> We're planning a training day tomorrow. Don't forget your laptops!

See what I mean?

Write in the second person

Quite simply, the words 'you', 'we' and 'us' are more inclined to invite readers in and create moments of connection. It's a quick and easy way to remind people that 'we're all in it together'. Also, try and make sure the word 'you' appears twice as much as 'we' and 'us'.

Don't write to impress

Making an obvious attempt at trying to impress is not appealing. Especially when the audience is hard at work and just trying to keep up with what's going on in between jobs. The focus should always be the reader and making it as quick and easy for them to understand as possible – so keep it as simple as you can.

A good yardstick is that if you don't use a word in natural conversation, avoid using it in your writing. Use a word that you would say instead. And keep your ears open – use words (the clean ones) that you hear being used around the workplace, because they're part of the common lingo of your audience, and using them can help you get heard.

Be less boring

Let's face it, some things are dull. Written policies, procedures and instructions are all boring things – a bit of a snoozefest in the reading department. But they are pretty important. And just as some companies have to sell mundane, yawn-triggering things like insurance or banking services (no offence), you can also find ways to 'sell' an organizational policy or procedure.

Research has shown that by including elements in your otherwise dreary content that are either inspiring, emotional, positive or surprising, your audience will not only respond to these accordingly, but be more likely to remember and share that experience with others regardless of how ordinary the topic is. So, if you want to create some social currency, it's a good thing to aim for.

You might be wondering how on earth to do that. For instance, how can you add a bit of pizzazz to get people's attention in a message about a change in health and safety policy? Here's a quick example:

New Message   • • •

To...

Subject: KISS-ing at work *latest news*

Keeping **I**t **S**afe and **S**ound

Every single one of you is important to us, and we like keeping you all safe and well so you can arrive home in the same condition you came to work – if not better! To keep to our word, we regularly check up on our written promise (otherwise known as our health and safety policy) and have spotted an opportunity to make it even better. You'll see this change helpfully highlighted for you in the attached revised policy document.

Give us the thumbs up to confirm you've both read and understood it by adding your name to page 6 before Friday 12th June. Any questions just email (me@mydesk. com).

Thanks everyone, have a great and safe day. #KISS

As you can see, rather than the subject header reading something like: 'Important – Changes to Health and Safety Policy' it offers a different way than expected to share this information.

If that feels a bit like too much of a stretch for your organization and not in line with how you want to sound, don't worry. It's just an example to illustrate a point, and you can apply your own employer voice that fits with the personality and tone you want to present.

And, of course, once you've got people's attention, you need to hold on to it and get people to take the final step – action! To speed this up, and as per the example, make sure you've not only provided the 'why' behind the message but also a clear call to action.

While we're on this subject, it's time for an exercise to see whether the boring scales tip in your favour or not:

Exercise: Spot check

What do your organizational procedures read like at the moment? Have a quick look at some of the procedural instructions that are floating around the workplace – either digitally or in print. Be on the lookout for things like unclear steps, inconsistency, hard to read formatting, lots of text and unnecessary (even redundant) information that could easily put people off or end up being misinterpreted. Do they pass the test of being clear and easy to understand and navigate, or are they making assumptions? Would a new recruit struggle? And are they even located in the right place where they're needed?

Keep it active not passive

Another pro technique is to always use 'active' not 'passive' language. It may sound unimportant and involves just a subtle change, but active sentences tend to make for stronger statements. Here's a few examples that show you how quick and easy it is to do:

Passive – 'A presentation was put together by the team for the meeting.'
Active – 'The team put a presentation together for the meeting.'

Passive – 'An award was won by our team.'
Active – 'Our team won an award.'

Passive – 'A new initiative is being planned.'
Active – 'We're planning a new initiative.'

Simple, subtle but somehow better.

DON'T SHOUT!

By this, I mean don't write in capitals. Not only is it 'SHOUTY!' and can come across as aggressive even if it's not meant to, it's actually proven to be more difficult to read because there's a lack of differentiation in the height and shape of the letters. Apparently, that's why things like road signs aren't in capitals – interesting.

Let's not be too harsh on capitals though. They DO serve a purpose in terms of emphasis. But use them SPARINGLY.

Pop the question

Get people interacting with their own thoughts as they read, by engaging them with questions. Have you noticed I've been doing this throughout the book? It's a simple, quick and genuine way to make readers feel more like they're getting involved in a meaningful two-way conversation.

Readability – formatting for clarity, convenience and impact

We're all lazy readers. We can't help it. Forever busy, with lots of distractions around us and random thoughts bobbing around in our minds, we've become a nation of scanners and skimmers.

When we're given something to read in whatever format (email, letter, brochure) we start asking questions straight away: 'what's this about?', 'is it worth reading?', for example. We'll be scanning to find the bits of information that are the most important to us, and at the same time looking for an excuse that justifies us filing it in the bin. Think about the way you read a report when it first lands on your desk, or that long email you've just received.

So, if something is immediately easy-on-the-eye and well formatted (e.g., the text is broken up with bits of white space or even the odd visual if appropriate) then the sender has already increased their chances of getting and holding your attention. Things like headers and subheaders allow people to digest the message in manageable chunks more easily. It sounds simple but formatting isn't always considered in the typical rush to get a message out.

Applying consistency of look and format across all of your written communications is a great way to help people take in information with less effort, and it has the added advantage of creating familiarity which in turn builds trust. And, a bonus for you, it also makes composing messages less mind-bending and faster which is exactly what your Tools of Engagement is going to help you to do. Everybody wins when a message is:

- easier to understand;
- doesn't cause reader fatigue;
- is aesthetically pleasing; and
- has simple navigation.

Talking of formatting, bullet lists are a great way of presenting information, and a top copywriting tip when using bullets is to always start with a strong point and end with a strong point. Most people assume that the last bullet is going to be the least important, so surprise them! Keep a strong point for the last bullet and if it's a good one, they'll notice it in a way that really helps to draw in all the other points on the list as well and make the message all the more memorable.

It's all in the detail

The best content comes from the realities of life – the granular detail and down-to-earth nitty gritty of day-to-day living. It's where the truth is. The small things that we all have experience of are what we relate to the most. Things that are organically part of daily life are what ring true and valid.

These details will sometimes reference good things, funny things and sometimes bad things. And that's fine because they're believable, it's what happens. We all have good days and bad days. Days when we stub a toe getting out of bed, get stuck in traffic on the way into work or realize we've forgotten to put the bin out (again).

If you think of those stand-up comics whose observational humour has us crying with laughter, it's because they're able to describe the tiny, silly things that we do or happen to us that we never mention but can all instantly relate to no matter who we are.

Adding little details into your internal comms can really help make a connection. Those seemingly insignificant bits of life that we all recognize, are an important part of the bonding process at work. In fact, researchers have found that the more familiar a story feels, the more powerful it is. So, it makes sense to incorporate some everyday truths into your comms to help you get your message across in a way that people identify with.

Avoiding word spam

Word spam can be described as anything that:

- is sloppy and lazy through lack of thought in content or format;
- doesn't have a clear point;

- hasn't provided any new information;
- hasn't considered the audience;
- is far too long and full of irrelevant detail;
- uses unnecessary jargon and 'big' words; or
- just doesn't make sense!

You know that cringy, squirmy feeling when you're listening to an awful, embarrassing presentation? You can't bring yourself to make eye contact. You're sitting there willing it to end, or planning your escape using the most inconspicuous moment to make a swift exit.

Or when you've picked up a report or article only to have to put it back down because it's literally too painful to read. And all because of bad writing.

'Think before you ink' is a good habit to get into, because people will thank you for sparing them from stuff like this:

> 'Strategic growth pivots on nurturing our workers to catalyze enterprises that yield success in our main markets. By prioritizing investment in our sector personnel, we foster specialists, forging teams aligned with our fundamental core principles. This approach fuels our dynamic expansion, as cultivated expertise and values-aligned collaborators empower the company to flourish in its areas of strength.'

Eh?

Beware of using buzz words that turn people off. For example, the words 'productivity' and 'efficiency' are pretty vital in terms of what they mean for the business, but they rarely have a personal meaning or emotional value for employees, leaving them with little or no connection to what you're saying. And as these words tend to be associated with 'work harder!' if they're not explained in a constructive way, they have a tendency to ring little alarm bells and put people on the defensive.

So, when you're putting a message together, think about the types of words and language that might unintentionally feed the great divide between employer and employees – the 'them and us'.

Another thing to avoid is taking a reader on a sight-seeing tour when there's a far more convenient direct route to the destination. We all know what a pain it is to receive a lengthy message only to find that just two of the eight paragraphs were of any relevance or use. Grrrr. Getting to the point as soon as you can is always a good idea and will be much appreciated by everyone. Think of the difference in the reading experience of an instruction manual versus a handy five-step guide. What would you rather read?

No matter the topic, a spammy message reads between the lines:

- 'I can't be bothered with you';
- 'I'm too busy with other things';
- 'you're not important';
- 'just work it out for yourselves'; or
- 'I don't want to be here either'.

And, of course, the response will be suitably lacking in return.

There's no getting around it. We reap what we sow when we communicate. Which means serving up meaningless, irrelevant and lazy messages is at best annoying and at worst, a whole waste of time.

Jargon

Something that's rarely appreciated is jargon.

The science of jargon has shown that using it is actually a sign of insecurity – it can signal anxiety and a need to display status when trying to impress. And that's interesting because in real life it actually does the opposite! And by virtue makes you far less relatable.

According to the Harvard Business Review's article *Does Your Office Have A Jargon Problem?*, organizational researchers used jargon to measure employee perceptions of 'bullshit' at their offices. And despite complaints and criticism of its pretentious and unnecessary nature (including believe it or not from industry and government leaders themselves!) jargon continues to enjoy the attributes of Teflon.

In the same article, the researchers describe one of their jargon studies involving two different groups of participants – one of high level and one of low-level professional status:

> 'Subjects were playing the role of researchers at a conference who were about to give a presentation to an audience. We gave them a choice of how to communicate, and this time, we asked them to explain their choice. Low-status participants again

preferred to use more jargon, and the explanations for their choice emphasized wanting to look good in the eyes of others. In the high-status condition, however, participants were more focused on communicating effectively and being understood clearly. In other words, the lower-status participants used more jargon because they were preoccupied with how they would be judged by others.'

People trip over long words and worse than that, it gives them an easy excuse to stop reading or listening. It's much better to make big or complicated concepts accessible and understandable by breaking them down and using basic vocabulary. You'll reap the rewards – and so will your readers.

A separate point to make is that jargon and slang are often used interchangeably even though they are different. Slang is informal and used in more social settings, whereas jargon is used more fundamentally in professional settings.

Just to add a caveat here. If you're talking about tech to technical people, then of course you need to use the right language for that situation. In this case, jargon redeems itself nicely and becomes acceptable terminology that helps to describe things precisely when simpler versions just don't exist.

Phrases from the corporate world can be pretty cringey as you can see here in this table. So, opt for plain English every time – it's free, accessible, relaxed and friendly. And most important of all – understandable!

Corporate jargon	Plain English
We're going to do a deep dive on this.	Let's make sure we understand the details so we can make the best decisions for everyone.
Go for the low hanging fruit.	Let's start with the easiest things first.
Synergy is key.	Doing it together is going to make this project easier and more enjoyable.
We need to leverage resources for more output.	How might we use what we've already got but in a different way, to achieve that goal?
We'll touch base next week.	I'll check in with you on Thursday to see how you're getting on.

The cost of jargon is real. It can make people feel excluded, communication more difficult and result in disengagement. Studies have also found that jargon 'can hurt impressions of a speaker; audiences often view these speakers as conniving, manipulative, or less likeable'. Not a good look for anyone.

If you want people to actively and willingly play their own individual parts and collectively help you drive growth, if you want to nurture talent and skills, if you want people to buy into what you're saying and doing, you need to understand what's important to them, respect their time and speak their language.

Headlines

We all love a good headline that draws our eye. But what we don't appreciate are gimmicks or misleading 'click-bait' hooks. It's all about getting the balance right.

Up for some insider information? Ok. There are nine time-tested headline types that copywriters use for getting a reader's attention – especially when they're first learning how to write a good one. It's worth knowing about these, especially as they can work well on the more 'hard-to-reach' individuals!

Here they are, demonstrated with some workplace examples.

Direct headlines

Direct headlines (as the name suggests) get straight to the point, without any attempt at cleverness or playfulness.

Workplace example: 'Staff car park – barrier will be unstuck by hometime!'

Indirect headlines

These headlines take a more subtle approach and use curiosity to raise a question in the reader's mind, which the main content of the message then answers.

Workplace example: 'Are you up for a challenge?'

News headlines

Pretty self-explanatory, news headlines announce something people are likely to be as yet unaware of.

Workplace example: 'We've been nominated for an award!'

'How to' headlines

A 'how to' headline can be very effective in its appeal to a particular audience.

Workplace example: 'How to save time claiming your expenses' – a more meaningful way of getting people to follow a new process that infers a direct benefit.

Question headlines

This kind of headline asks the type of question that empathizes with the reader straight away, making them want to read on and see it answered. It raises curiosity while implying there's a solution in the content.

Workplace example: 'Are you missing the opportunity to reduce your workload?'

Command headlines

A command headline boldly tells the reader what they need to do. The trick here is that the first word should be a strong verb demanding action.

Workplace example: 'Grab your ticket to this year's Summer BBQ. There's a sausage with your name on it!'

Reasons why headlines

Another good one is the 'reason why' headline. Like the question headline, you can use a situation to spark a desire for the answer, which you then provide in the content.

Workplace example: 'The reason why you'll see more visitors on site this week.'

Number headlines

Numbers often work in headlines because people are attracted to predictability over uncertainty. The presence of a number creates an expectation that helps readers know what's in store – it's the promise of something specific.

Workplace example: 'Three ways to enhance your pension plan.'

Testimonial headlines

The testimonial headline provides proof from another source that supports the content of your message.

Workplace example: 'Reed It and Weep are our top supplier – friendly, reliable and always on time. *B. Tidy, Procurement Manager at Box-it Ltd*'

Swipe file

Something you might find helpful is a 'swipe file', a much-loved resource in the copywriting world. A swipe file is a list of words or phrases that help prompt you when you can't quite think of a better word or way to say or describe something. Listed under certain subject or scenario headings for easy reference, there are lots of swipe-file sources online that you can refer to or download. They can be really handy for helping you avoid the dreaded word repetition and writers block symptoms.

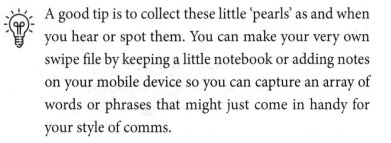

A good tip is to collect these little 'pearls' as and when you hear or spot them. You can make your very own swipe file by keeping a little notebook or adding notes on your mobile device so you can capture an array of words or phrases that might just come in handy for your style of comms.

Using visuals

Just because this book is about communicating through words doesn't mean you should discount using visuals as well.

In fact, educational researchers have found that 83% of human learning occurs visually. As humans, we actually think in pictures. So, including images that help you 'tell a story' or explain something that might be a bit more complex can be a really good idea.

When words are chosen well, they conjure up images in a reader's mind – like a familiar connection. That's why people love the convenience of emojis – they communicate emotions and situations in a simple, immediate way. But we can't really just rely on emojis at work! 😆

Infographics, images, icons and symbols can make a great contribution to your internal comms and help share and encourage ideas. Visual appeal plus persuasive wording can be a powerful thing – you see it used in advertising all the time, on everything from billboards to buses.

In the workplace, the potential for using visuals is far ranging – from explaining instructions and presenting facts to calling people to action. And used considerately and in a consistent way, they can create a common 'visual language' that speeds up understanding.

In any communication, you want to be building rapport, establishing trust and creating a stronger connection. And because visuals allow people to see the same information in different ways, they can be particularly persuasive when used in conjunction with the right words, language and tone.

Storytelling

This is such a cool topic that it gets a main section of its own.

Humans are wired to respond to stories. When we hear a good story, the electrical impulses in our brains light up, firing up multiple neurons at the same time (dull facts and boring stories not so much). And neuroscientists have found that when this happens, these fired-up neurons fuse themselves together, which then creates lasting triggers for us to remember the story afterwards. It's one of the reasons why content marketers use storytelling in their work. The other reason is that stories trigger the release of oxytocin – aka 'the love drug'. So, stories make us remember and they make us care. Ahh, nice.

So, if you want people to engage with your message, make them part of the story (non-fiction of course). Storytelling is really powerful and a fantastic way to create narrative, flow and connection – they can be short and sweet, and you don't need to start with a 'once upon a time', or end with 'happily ever after'.

But, what do we mean by story and how does storytelling have a place in internal comms?

A story has a start, a middle and an end, so it takes people on a journey of steps, stages, chapters – each following on from the last to keep people hooked and wanting to know what happens next. Even the briefest of stories have these elements.

People love to know where they fit into a story. We don't like to be left out.

Some examples of where you can use storytelling in the workplace include:

- sharing the vision and values;
- communicating change and transformation;
- recognizing and celebrating achievements;
- creating a sense of community; and
- training and sharing knowledge.

Donald Miller, in his brilliant book 'Building A Storybrand' sets out his seven-part framework (SB7) which reveals and demonstrates the fundamental formula, involving a hero and a guide, that's used in *every* successful movie you can think of.

I've referred to his framework here in this table for comparison, to show how the story formula relates not just to movies, but to marketing and also the workplace.

Donald Miller's SB7 framework	Movie example (*Star Wars: Episode IV*)	Marketing example	Workplace example
↓ 1. A character (the hero)	Luke Skywalker	Customer	Employee
↓ 2. Has a problem	Needs to destroy the Death Star	Needs to buy birthday gift for friend	Needs to write a report but not sure how
↓ 3. And meets a guide	Obi-Wan Kenobi	Shop assistant	Manager
↓ 4. Who gives them a plan	Become a Jedi	Shows the latest gadget, ideally priced	Provides a helpful template and checklist
↓ 5. And calls them to action	Use the Force	Buy now and get a free personalized case	Follow this guide
↓ 6. That helps them avoid failure	Destroys the Death Star and becomes a Jedi	Can give friend great gift both practical and personal	Report finished on time to a high quality
7. And ends in success	Avoids defeat/ capture by Darth Vader	Customer is happy, friend is delighted	Task completed successfully, manager-employee relationship strengthened

Simple but definite parallels.

By way of contrast, there's a lot of communication going on in organizations that amounts to poor and uninspiring storytelling, and however well-meaning the intention, creates the opposite response to the one hoped for.

Here's a real-life example.

It involves a visit I made to a multi-site, international manufacturing company where the Senior Ops Director was explaining how frustrated he was that day.

This was because earlier on, he and the MD had addressed a group of middle managers to share the new company vision and update them on progress. They were expecting to inspire and motivate people with this exciting news. Except it hadn't quite had the desired effect.

They'd presented a professionally made video about the new, ten-year vision. I asked what was in it. He showed me. I watched the whole 20 minutes. There was definitely a story there. It evolved through a timeline, starting with when the company was founded (1923 if you're interested), mapping key achievements along the way. And eventually the story led through to the more recent rise of its global success enjoyed today (much evidenced via graphs and pie charts as well as imagery of sun-kissed plant machinery against a blue sky) and then ended by taking us into the future vision of even more growth through acquisition – *just checking you're still awake?*

Anyway, I asked if he and the MD had made any reference to the employees and what was going to be happening on their particular site. Oh yes, he said. As well as the film, they'd presented some site-specific data slides showing the site's excellent health and safety record but also the need for an 18% increase in efficiency across the operation in the next two years – but that last 'bit' of information will be covered in more detail another time as they didn't want to overwhelm the managers with too much info.

Hmm. Let's look at the missing elements of that story:

- The hero was the company, not the audience.

- The problem is not clear.

- The guides did not provide a plan for solving said problem.

- There was no call to action.

- Failure is therefore very much an option.

- It ends in confusion (and lot of time wasted).

This is one of many examples of a bad story, poorly communicated to an audience whose needs hadn't been considered – and whose overriding takeaway from the whole thing was worrying news about efficiencies to take back to the other guys on the shopfloor. The negative fallout from that was pretty epic as you can imagine, and there was pressure for a better 'sequel' to put things right.

Every organization is full of stories unfolding constantly, which if captured and used well in your comms, can do much to capture imagination and connect people, purpose and strategy in a relatable way. But you need to be intentional about it. Many storytelling opportunities aren't recognized as such so try to keep your eyes and ears open for possibilities.

Every scene tells a story

It's not just words and pictures that help tell a story. The physical working environment plays its part too.

Visually – and in terms of overall experience – what would you say your physical workplace looks and feels like right now? When a person comes to visit and takes a walk around, have you ever wondered (or asked) what impression they get or what perception they might leave with?

If this person happened to be a potential customer or client, it's quite an important thing to consider, and maybe you do that quite well already. Or perhaps you don't get visitors, so whatever the environment might reveal about you, your people and the business overall isn't really a priority as such.

Either way, of course, it does matter to the people *in* the business who walk through the door every day to do their jobs. Jobs that sometimes, as we all know and can relate to, can be challenging for various reasons – such as a peak in workload, the complexity of a project or indeed change and uncertainty.

Just like verbal communication, not all of the message comes from the words spoken. Body language contributes with its incredibly telling non-verbal cues that hint at the underlying truth. The same thing applies to the physical workplace – it tells a story, or at the very least provides an interesting narrative of its own.

In terms of scenery, we're not just talking about the standard of aesthetics and orderliness here, though what's not to like about an attractive and well-organized workplace. You only have to look at the effort that some organizations are making (and not just cash-rich companies) to create a more inviting place to work. We spend long enough there earning our money, so it's not beyond the rainbow to think about making it a nicer place to be.

No, we're also talking about the cues we get from the wording and visuals on signs, posters and notice boards across offices, workstations, corridors, social areas and meeting rooms. These add to the narrative more subtly than direct communication, and can affect people both consciously and subliminally.

With potential for influence over time, the best kind of physical cues are positive and productive ones that align with the kind of workplace and experience people want to be part of.

But who paints this picture? Who is the Michelangelo of your organization? Being in charge means you're one of the lead architects of the work environment that people experience. You can't do it alone, but you can influence the brief for others to follow.

So, when you're looking to improve internal communication, it's worth remembering that the stuff that gets hung on walls, pinned on boards or painted on the ground play their part. The odds stack more in everyone's favour when the physical space reflects the positive culture you're nurturing with your internal comms.

Try this exercise and *see* what you find.

Exercise: The look-see audit

Take an eyes-wide-open look around. You could ask a few different people to accompany you so you get a feel, from those valuably different perspectives, for what these physical cues are saying. They could be good, bad or indifferent. Bad or indifferent ones need attention – get rid or replace. Some may have been there for so long that they're obsolete or more recently out of date.

Some of the offenders could be curling up at their crisp, brown edges, maybe dangling lopsided so you have to be intrigued enough to stop in your tracks and tilt your head to one side to read them. Perhaps old news is still peeking out obstinately behind the latest version of something. These things might be beautifully laminated but no longer relevant, or lovingly formatted but be absolutely diddly squat of value. If you conclude that they really don't matter and have no purpose, why are they there? And as for the things that are seen as good, once you've tackled the bad and indifferent, why not replicate more of the good or even turn it into great.

This can be a really insightful and enlightening thing to do, inspiring a whole new way of thinking about the physical and visual side of communication in your organization.

Talking of which…

I spy – the art of observation

Working in business improvement meant visiting lots of different business sites up and down the country. I quickly learned the 'drive by' technique. This involved using all the visual cues – or should that be clues – in line of sight, to help me prepare mentally, and strategically, for the meeting ahead. Let me explain.

I soon realized that you can quickly glean, from what you see with your own eyes, the essence or culture of a business and how it's run. We're more inclined to believe what we see rather than what we're told, especially if the two aren't immediately in sync.

It can start as soon as you arrive. If the car parking spaces nearest to the building's entrance door have painted signs that say 'Reserved for Directors only' or words to that effect, what would you think about the style and attitude of its leadership?

If the reception was unmanned, and it took you several minutes to work out from a set of grubby instructions (laid next to a dead potted plant) that you need to use a rather dirty looking telephone to signal your arrival – and even then it took ages for someone to answer, looking annoyed when they come down the stairs – how would you feel?

Whereas, if you came onto site and there was no hierarchy for parking spaces, you're greeted with a warm welcome sign and right in front of you is a shiny clean telephone with a two-step guide for alerting someone who says hi with a smile – it's a different experience altogether. One that simply says, without fuss, fanfare or massive cost, we value people.

As children we're often told 'do as you would be done by' which is a virtuous value to live by. It's a shame that this sensibility can get lost so deeply in the 'grown-up' cut and thrust world of business and work.

In summary, when it comes to being a communication pro, don't neglect the physical environment because it really can help you create the right conditions for improving engagement and connection.

Chapter 13

Measuring impact

Defining and acknowledging the value of IC is one thing, measuring it is another.

When the practice of internal communication isn't recognized as a key management function embedded into the core business model, it's likely that as a management tool, it isn't specifically discussed at leadership or board level as part of the running agenda. If this is the case, it won't be seen as something to evaluate.

However, operational, commercial and people problems will definitely be topics of debate in those meeting rooms. And because we know that most of these issues are a result of poor communication, then inadvertently IC makes its way into every discussion at every level of the organization by default.

For organizations who want to make improvements, ideally there needs to be a way of evaluating whether or not their internal comms are making a positive difference. But what is a 'positive' difference?

The higher you go in a company hierarchy, the greater the focus there'll be on the return on investment of anything that has used money and time. So, if internal communication was to feature on the agenda, there's going to be at least some consideration of its return on investment (ROI). Which is fair enough of course. The appropriate use of money and the generating of profit is pretty key to an organization's success!

But, the danger of focusing only on the more typical and financially driven metrics for IC is that assessment of its success or failure is going to focus more on outputs than outcomes.

In his ground-breaking book, *The Advantage*, Patrick Lencioni talks about the three biases that affect organizations, concluding that most companies – being suspicious of 'touchy-feely stuff' – don't embrace simpler and more accessible tactics to create organizational health and happy employees. And by virtue of being traditionally too busy focusing on things which are sophisticated (complex), adrenaline fuelled (high effort) and quantifiable (can be analysed financially) they are missing the humble but majorly significant value of some rather more basic principles.

Like good communication for instance.

Evaluation – safety in numbers?

The success of internal comms is typically measured via retention rates, response rates to internal surveys, attendance at company events, engagement with internal digital platforms (usually meaning clicks) and productivity. But what is it that this kind of data is not telling us? Let's take them one by one.

Retention rates – These are quite helpful in a broad sense, but don't offer the answer to 'why' an employee has chosen to leave and go elsewhere, unless the numbers are accompanied by meaningful exit interview responses. And if you don't know why, you haven't got the information to know how you can start putting things right to avoid more loss.

Survey response rates – Indicating the number of responses generated at a particular point in time, these figures tell you little without the insight from the *content* of the responses. Which brings us on to the quality of the questions. For a survey to be of value, what do you *really* need to know and understand? What's important for both the day to day and overall success of the business?

According to the IC Index 2023 report, UK workers are more positive about their employer's attitude towards open and honest feedback when they run an annual survey as part of wider listening. As might be expected, the worst thing employers can do is to not do any listening at all.

Surveys designed with the right questions and objectives are a convenient tool for gathering information in bulk, but it's generally agreed that it's impossible for them to provide the entire picture. While they can help to set benchmarks and satisfy the need for figures, standalone they don't offer the nuances and subtleties of the whole in-your-face reality of what's happening day to day in those meeting rooms, corridors or cafeterias.

Attendance at work social events – As an indication of how engaged and enthusiastic someone is, this is somewhat flawed. People can feel compelled to 'join in' because of peer pressure or looking bad in front of the boss. I've experienced this myself, back when I was a disengaged employee, so counting my involvement as a sign of engagement would have been skewed.

Use of internal digital platforms – This data is questionable. In reality, some people won't be confident enough to use them, others will overuse them and annoy people (you know the ones) and most people are probably too busy to be opening up another tab on their screens to add yet another series of conversations to their day. It's really *what's* being said and shared on the digital platforms that's going to be of use.

Productivity – More closely related to ROI is productivity, as defined and measured by the nature and KPIs of each unique business. But how do you measure the link between productivity and internal communication? A research article called 'Analysing the relationship between productivity and human communication in an organizational setting' reports that:

> 'While these studies [employee surveys and questionnaires] are useful, they can be challenged on the grounds that perceptions of communication do not correspond to actual communication behavior... Direct observation is the "gold standard" for measuring communication and provides the most rigorous test of the communication-productivity relationship.' – PLOS ONE, July 2021 (Authors: Arindam Dutta, Elena Steiner, Jeffrey Proulx, Visar Berisha, Daniel W. Bliss, Scott Poole, Steven Corman)

It's good to know that observation is officially up there when it comes to credible evaluation of the impact of communication on productivity.

So how does all this measurement stuff add up?

Evidence from the numbers may throw up some hidden surprises (good or bad) for those not involved in the day to day, but for the people on the ground it's likely that the data just confirms what they've already concluded through observation, experience and feelings.

In summary, it's understandable to overvalue numbers and undervalue (or ignore) anything difficult to quantify – for the simple reason it's easier! While data and measurement are crucial in any organization, it needs to be considered in relation to the more qualitative thoughts, attitudes and behaviours of the people involved. The things you see people do and don't do on a daily basis.

What's your instinctive 'gut feeling' from what you observe as you walk around the place? Listen too. What are the most common issues HR are dealing with? How much firefighting is going on? Where are mistakes being made or misunderstandings happening? And so on.

You can look out for signs of how things are panning out on the ground in relation to the organization's purpose, goals, vision and values. Are they aligned? Do people know what they are? Do they care?

And never underestimate your own observation, judgement and instinct over a big pile of stats. What's more, by the time you've waded through that pile, analysed the numbers, written up the report and waited for any resulting conclusions, it's likely that the goal posts on the ground have shifted once again. It's often better to get a rough answer to the right question than a detailed answer to the wrong or redundant question.

Once you're more in tune with the 'mood music' you'll have more insight from different perspectives to use in your comms planning. And if you have those intuitive feedback loops (calls to action) continually working for you within your internal comms, you'll have also had the advantage of gauging the mood on a regular basis. Timely info!

Next, we're going to look at how you build in a systematic IC review process that fits into regular meeting activity, to avoid the risk of your internal comms and its progress slipping down the priority pole.

Reviewing progress

In capturing your organization's DNA – its plans, aspirations, values and so on – your Tools of Engagement Framework becomes an asset. And like any asset it needs optimizing and looking after.

The main objective is to keep it alive, fresh and current as part of regular company practice – just like you do with budgets or training, for example. So, find what works best for you and your team, get it in the diary and keep showing up.

For convenience, using your already scheduled and regular meetings, add IC as a standing agenda item so you've systematically created a frequent time and opportunity to discuss and review (even briefly) the roll-out of the latest comms. This is a good way to get into the discipline of using IC as a management tool, noting progress and feedback, making adjustments such as a change of emphasis if needed, and staying consistent.

Or, if you prefer, you could schedule regular stand-alone review meetings for IC – but keep the agenda tight as you don't want it turning into something else. Stay *communication* focused. If something sends you off-piste, note it as an unwelcome gatecrasher and a matter to be carried forward to a more appropriate forum.

Your reviews will naturally flag up news of progress that you can feedback into your internal comms. It should be evident that you're listening to feedback and providing updates or follow-ons.

It's good to remember that every communication builds on the previous one, and each is a step in the right direction. No one single message will transform the business, but with consistency, positive changes start to happen. Results are hardly ever immediate, but when effort is being made to give everyone a tangible sense of progress, it's easier to keep their focus on the journey rather than purely on the destination.

Supporting other communicators

Line managers, team leaders and supervisors are often the first in line to field questions from employees, making them key communicators too. So, when you're planning on making an announcement or rolling out a new initiative for instance, always be sure to provide them with a heads up, and if possible a few additional details ahead of time.

Helping them prepare for any potential questions they might get asked, and giving them an opportunity to provide their teams with some extra information is both the right and smart thing to do. You'll not only be supporting them in confidence, understanding and credibility, you'll be strengthening your working relationship and making your job easier at the same time. And as an added bonus, you'll know with welcome reassurance that you're all sharing a single, unified message at each level of the company.

A force for good

However you decide to evaluate your Tools of Engagement Framework, it's going to appreciate in value every time it's used and built on. You'll be gaining momentum and traction with each clear, consistent and purposeful message you put out there.

Your employees will start to sense an upward shift in their level of connection and involvement in the organization now that the dots are being joined and the story makes more sense.

Through more considered internal comms, your people will benefit from:

- Enjoying a better understanding of their individual role, contribution and what's needed from them.
- Feeling better informed so they can work more positively, confidently and cooperatively on a daily basis.
- Seeing and feeling the company values being put into action.
- Being more open to new ways of learning and growing in their role, and supporting others.

 As you get more confident, look for contact points with your employees that you haven't explored yet that could be worth harnessing as an opportunity for great communication and connection (not forgetting the physical environment itself).

Let your Tools of Engagement take a seat at the decision-making table whenever you're strategizing, planning and preparing to communicate. It makes a fine starting point and an even better compass.

Chapter 14

Time for reflection

We've covered a lot of ground together. I think you deserve some quiet time to look back and reflect.

Knowledge is a wonderful thing. It expands our awareness and increases our understanding of ourselves and others. But without putting it into practice and applying the learning for everyone's benefit, it stays filed under 'stuff I know' and makes no real difference.

You've taken the time to read this book, so it makes sense to now reflect and think about your own experiences that may resonate – or perhaps conflict – with what you've read and learned.

It's important that you develop your own natural style of communicating. Your Tools of Engagement Framework will help you significantly with making internal comms an easier, more efficient and worthwhile process. And the great thing is that within it you'll find your own way of doing things.

The subject

Having immersed yourself in the topic of internal communication, where in this book have new thoughts been triggered or provided confirmation and justification of what you already knew or suspected? Equally, where has your thinking been challenged?

Analysing and understanding

What concepts stood out to you? Which examples resonated the most? How did the ideas relate to your own experiences and values? Think about some of the challenges and scenarios we've covered and how they measure up with any of your own organizational dynamics right now.

Identifying lessons

What are the key lessons or takeaways from this book for you? Did you do the exercises? Which of the practical tools, tips and techniques could enhance your workplace? And how might the underpinning knowledge of what makes people tick influence how you communicate and build productive relationships from now on?

When you want to understand your audience so that you're empowered to say and do the right things, try using these questions:

- What problem are we trying to solve here?
- Who is it that's having the problem?
- What opportunity are we trying to jump on?
- What might or could this opportunity mean to our people?
- What could we do or say to help realize this opportunity?
- What would make people want to be part of it?
- How can we encourage them to take part in it?
- What do we want them to think or feel?
- What do they need to know in order to align action with what's needed?

Asking these kinds of questions, of yourself and others, takes you beyond just reading this book. They help you soak up the concepts and consider how they can positively impact you, the people you work with and the business. And by default, you get yourself some rich intel through the answers!

Confident communication

Confidence usually comes with knowledge and experience. And that works equally for leaders, managers and employees alike. In fact, for everyone, young and old. We're all learning, gathering know-how and experience as we go, and correcting ourselves when needed along the way. Our level of confidence in any given situation comes through in what we think, say and do.

As a people manager you're taking steps to build and strengthen your confidence as an effective communicator so you can offer the very best support to others. This is going to involve being curious and increasing your awareness and understanding of what's going on around you.

So, it's good to have a few guiding thought processes to turn to when you find yourself in a situation where people are looking to you for guidance.

- Keep asking questions of yourself and others.
- Focus on solutions – how might we make this work?
- Stay open, positive and approachable.
- Keep looking for new learning and better ways to do (and communicate!) things.
- Think about the different ways you can use your new understanding and knowledge.
- Stay accountable to your own thoughts, emotions and actions.

Planning for the future

And now you get to take action by applying good communication practice in your workplace. What goals will you set? Perhaps it'll be more engaging content, encouraging more feedback or improving information flow between teams and departments.

Will you initiate some fresh thinking? You could kick-off your refreshed comms by focusing on something specific that's going on or will be happening soon.

This is your opportunity to make good comms happen with the kind of messaging that:

- connects people with each other for a purpose;
- invites (and gets) meaningful participation; and
- embraces creativity, not limits.

So, grab that pen or reach for that keyboard – you're about to be brilliant!

Chapter 15

To be continued...

You'll have guessed by now that this is not a traditional leadership or management manual!

It doesn't seek to question or replace your business or people strategy. Its purpose is to help you optimize all the existing opportunities within your organization while taking into account future plans and challenges, and provides an actionable plan to support you and your people through the powerful platform of internal communication.

If you feel refreshed or have been inspired in any way by what you've read, it doesn't have to stop here. Yes, you've rumbled me – here come *my* calls to action!

Whether you decide to make a few adjustments to improve your current internal comms or go ahead and create your own unique Tools of Engagement Framework, you can enjoy more insight, know-how and news from the official website www.refreshingcomms.co.uk where you'll find:

- downloadable resources for self-learning;
- blogs and news; and
- workshop and coaching options.

And while you're at it why not join the growing *Refreshing Comms* community. Simply sign up on the website to have a 'Wave of Inspiration' hit your inbox every now and then – straight from me to you.

Or you could just drop me a message and tell me how the book has influenced you. You know how I value feedback!

Whatever you do next, please continue to be inspired by the opportunities for further advancing your own development, your organization and the people you work with through better communication, and make your Tools of Engagement Framework a cornerstone of how the business operates – adapting and building on it over the coming months and years.

That way, you and those around you can enjoy the refreshing experience of a better connected, feel good, goal-achieving workplace.

Enjoy the gift of communication!

A special call to action

I must confess, I haven't quite finished with you yet. I feel a revolution coming on.

Refreshing Comms is on a quest to encourage employers to create a small space on site for a 'life library' where anyone in the organization – employees, managers and leaders alike – can share, swap, borrow, discuss and read great books.

With a focus on books that inspire both personal and professional development, and which challenge thinking and impart new knowledge, your life library will be a great work community resource with oodles of potential for creating opportunities and growth on individual, team and organizational levels.

As well as being a great, easily accessible place to exercise the old grey matter more creatively and spontaneously, it's also going to boost:

- wellbeing;
- workplace experience;
- ideas;
- knowledge and awareness;
- conversations;
- collaboration;
- equality, diversity and inclusion; and
- innovation.

It's the words in books, the thinking triggered and the learning that follows that lead to new ideas and better understanding of ourselves and others. So where better to have them accessible than in the workplace itself where communication and conversation can be used so powerfully.

As a simple and humble idea (you could even just start with a few books on a shelf) it could quickly and easily become a reality in any workplace that values people and knowledge – so why not do it? You might be surprised at its success.

Invite people to recommend or bring in books they've read or been inspired by to add to the mix. There are so many things you can do creatively off the back of your library initiative.

For those of you who choose to take on this friendly challenge, I salute you. Tell me about your life library. Send me pics. And above all make the most of what's fully available and accessible to you and your people: the words, wisdom and fresh thinking of others!

> 'Employ your time in improving yourself by other men's writings, so that you shall gain easily what others have labored hard for.' – Socrates

A quick word on AI and communication

Before I sign off, I thought it'd be a bit remiss of me not to mention AI, in particular ChatGPT. After all, you might be thinking that this new technology is going to be a far quicker and more efficient way of 'writing' internal comms. In which case you'll consider me a bit of a crazy fool for even bothering to write this book if tech has got the future of communication covered.

Well, you could definitely give it a go. Maybe you already have?! You'd need to feed in quite a bit of detailed information for it to produce something anywhere near customized. Even so, you might still find yourself having to do a bit of editing.

Now, writer I am, philosopher I'm not. So, just a quick word on this. Not quick because I think artificial intelligence applied as a writing tool hasn't got its uses – it certainly has and it's going to be absolutely fascinating to see how the technology advances – but quick because even as I write, it'll be changing and evolving every minute. So, whatever I say about it now will soon become purely academic.

At the moment, it appears from the general chit chat around that the jury is out – there's no consensus and it's a bit of a crowd divider (think Marmite and Brexit). It's certainly sorting the 'purists' from the more tech hungry consumers.

Interestingly, AI-generated communication is happening at a time when workforce surveys and skill improvement plans are highlighting the biggest cross-cutting skill gap of new recruits – and indeed the general workforce – as guess what...? Yep, written and verbal communication. And within this, employers point to a frustrating lack of interpersonal skills, soft skills, emotional intelligence and team problem-solving. Thought for the day perhaps.

In terms of human-to-human communication, and the art of engaging and influencing others through feelings and emotions (which as we now know rule us all) I'm not convinced AI will readily provide the kind of comms we need – the kind that has the authenticity and soul that comes from the lived experience and weirdly wonderful nuanced truths of that thing we call the workplace.

So, for now, I'll keep writing.

#iamnotarobot

Acknowledgements

Any author knows that you don't write a book in isolation. It might feel a tad lonely at the time, but then you look back and realize that it's other people who have kept you going. So, where do you start with gratitude when you've got so much of it?

Nige – Just when you thought it was safe and the HRT had finally kicked in, your menopausal partner decided to write a book – sorry about that. But just like you've always done and continue to do, you're there by my side. Thanks for sticking with me on what was yet another emotional journey!

My daughter Holly – This wouldn't and couldn't haven't happened at all if it wasn't for you. Not only did you invite me to join the business, you've encouraged my creation of *Refreshing Comms* and the writing of it every single day. You made it fun, rallied my spirits and kept me going in every sense of the word.

My son Tom – Your support and encouragement has boosted my confidence so often while I was writing. The thought and effort I see you put into your own career and learning has always impressed and inspired me, and always will.

My grandchildren Finch and Artie – The loves of my life, my little guys. Every smile, every laugh and every cuddle was needed! Keep reading and writing, boys. Never stop learning and above all stay curious. It'll serve you well.

My sister Christine – For being proud of me for doing this, and reminding me how proud mum and dad would have been too, thanks big sis.

And along the way…

Phil Teasdale and Lucy Patterson - Thank you both for introducing me to Design Thinking which helped me bring my book and business ideas to life. You both triggered something in me, and I really enjoy and appreciate having your friendship and support.

Alison Jones and the Practical Inspiration Publishing team - Taking me from 'could I really write an actual book?' to being a published author. Thank you.

Throughout my research, I've followed and studied the expertise and thinking of leading voices in the internal communications and HR profession whose work I admire enormously. Special thanks to Jenni Field for providing the foreword, and to Perry Timms, Jennifer Sproul, Katie Macaulay and Cat Barnard for their individual endorsements of *Refreshing Comms*. I've also had the pleasure of a lively call with Bill Quirke. I truly appreciate every one of you for giving me your time and sharing your wisdom.

And James @cjwarwood - Your illustrations are just perfect, and your service was impeccable. Thank you for using your creative talent to add to the fun side of this book and for bringing my concepts and characters to life.

About the author

Liz Atkin is Director of the award-winning, brand copywriting studio Blonde Creative based in Teesside, and an internal comms strategist who has spent her career using the power of words to positively influence people and inspire action. She lives in the seaside town of Redcar in the glorious North East of England.

Her own experience as CEO of an organization transitioning through change while harbouring a toxic culture gave her first-hand insight into the way that internal communication can make or break a business.

She went on to spend ten years working in the manufacturing industry assessing operational and workplace culture issues, advising MDs and senior managers in operations and HR, and providing solutions through training and consultancy.

Liz now combines her business experience, communication expertise and creative thinking to help businesses of all types across the UK and internationally to engage with their target audiences – external and internal – through strategic positioning, powerful narrative and authentic messaging.

Always keen to connect and work with others who share a vision of a better workplace, Liz also delivers coaching, training and consultancy for those in search of a Refresh!

Connect with Liz:

linkedin.com/in/liz-atkin-4400a9250

liz@blondecreative.co.uk

www.refreshingcomms.co.uk

Index

A quick word from Practical Inspiration Publishing...

We hope you found this book both practical and inspiring – that's what we aim for with every book we publish.

We publish titles on topics ranging from leadership, entrepreneurship, HR and marketing to self-development and wellbeing.

Find details of all our books at: www.practicalinspiration.com

Did you know...

We can offer discounts on bulk sales of all our titles – ideal if you want to use them for training purposes, corporate giveaways or simply because you feel these ideas deserve to be shared with your network.

We can even produce bespoke versions of our books, for example with your organization's logo and/or a tailored foreword.

To discuss further, contact us on info@practicalinspiration.com.

Got an idea for a business book?

We may be able to help. Find out more about publishing in partnership with us at: bit.ly/PIpublishing.

Follow us on social media...

 @PIPTalking

 @pip_talking

 @practicalinspiration

@piptalking

Practical Inspiration Publishing